Assumptions Harden Into Facts

The Book

Compiled & Edited
by
David Allen

Published by Shanon Allen
Copyright © 2016

Legal

Copyright © 2016 by Shanon Allen

All rights reserved. No part of this publication may be reproduced, duplicated, distributed, or transmitted in any form or by any means, including photocopying, recording, or other electronic or mechanical methods, without the prior written permission of the publisher, except in the case of brief quotations embodied in critical reviews and certain other noncommercial uses permitted by copyright law.

Printed in the United States of America

First Printing

ISBN: 978-0-9972801-6-6

Visit Us At **NevilleGoddardBooks.com** for a complete listing of all our books and **1000's of Free Books to Read online and download.**

Introduction

From The Power of Awareness

The study of this book, with its detailed exposition of consciousness and the operation of the law of assumption, is the master key to the conscious attainment of your highest destiny.

This very day start your new life.

Approach every experience in a new frame of mind, with a new state of consciousness. Assume the noblest and the best for yourself in every respect and continue therein.

Make believe . . great wonders are possible.

Editors Notes

This Neville Goddard companion book is simply a focused compilation of his teachings on the Law of Assumption. By compiling certain teachings into one book I feel it helps the reader who desires to focus on one teaching over another. This has been my goal in compiling his works.

Those who are not quite as familiar with Neville Goddard might find it helpful to know what he taught, prior to diving into his readings. Imagination and The Law of Assumption, to me, are his main teachings. This is why I have chosen to give my attention to these two important aspects of his work, in two separate works, this, Assumptions Harden Into Facts: The Book and Imagination: The Redemptive Power in Man. Both are very valuable teachings.

While there are many Neville Goddard books available, I wanted to condense, into single books, what I feel is important and also make these specific teachings easier to focus on, for the reader, rather than having to search through all his material to find what you are looking for.

I feel I have accomplished that.

David Allen

Neville Goddard

Learn the art of assumption, for only in this way can you create your own happiness.

The Assumption is the crown of the mysteries because it is the highest use of consciousness.

Directory

      Legal
      Introduction
      Editors Notes
7   122 Individual quotes from Neville's books and lectures
89   4 Lectures on The Law of Assumption:
90   Lecture 1 of 4 - Persistent Assumption . . 03-18-1968
98   Lecture 2 of 4 - Persistent Assumption . . 06-18-1968
116 Lecture 3 of 4 - You Dare To Assume . . 06-19-1970
133 Lecture 4 of 4 - Radio Talk - The Law of Assumption
140 Neville's Case Histories:
141 Case History 1
144 Case History 2
148 Case History 3
151 Case History 4
153 Case History 5
155 Case History 6
157 Case History 7
159 Case History 8
162 Neville discusses failure in the attempted use of The Law of Assumption
166 Books by David Allen
167 Suggested Reading

122 Individual quotes from Neville's books and lectures, on The Law of Assumption

1.

The whole of creation is asleep within the deep of man and is awakened to objective existence by his subconscious assumptions.

2.

Subjective words . . subconscious assumptions . . awaken what they affirm.

They are living and active

and

*"shall not return unto me void,
but shall accomplish that which I please,
and shall prosper in the thing whereto I sent them."*

3.

Man creates himself out of his own imagination.

If the state desired is for yourself and you find it difficult to accept as true what your senses deny, call before your mind's eye the subjective image of a friend and have him mentally affirm that you are already that which you desire to be.

This establishes in him, without his conscious consent or knowledge, the subconscious assumption that you are that which he mentally affirmed, which assumption, because it is unconsciously assumed, will persist until it fulfills its mission.

Its mission is to awaken in you, its vibratory correlate, which vibration, when awakened in you, realizes itself as an objective fact.

4.

That which requires a state of consciousness to produce its effect obviously cannot be effected without such a state of consciousness, and in your ability to assume the feeling of a greater life, to assume a new concept of yourself, you possess what the rest of Nature does not possess . . imagination . . the instrument by which you create your world.

Your imagination is the instrument, the means, whereby your redemption from slavery, sickness, and poverty is effected.

If you refuse to assume the responsibility of the incarnation of a new and higher concept of yourself, then you reject the means, the only means, whereby your redemption, that is, the attainment of your ideal, can be effected.

Imagination is the only redemptive power in the universe.

5.

We must act on the assumption that we already possess that which we desire, for all that we desire is already present within us. It only waits to be claimed. That it must be claimed is a necessary condition by which we realize our desires.

Our prayers are answered if we assume the feeling of the wish fulfilled and continue in that assumption.

6.

What we are conscious of is constructed out of what we are not conscious of. Not only do our subconscious assumptions influence our behavior but they also fashion the pattern of our objective existence. They alone have the power to say,

> *"Let us make man . . objective manifestations . . in our image, after our likeness."*

7.

If you assume that you are what you want to be your desire is fulfilled, and in fulfillment all longing is neutralized. You cannot continue desiring what you have already realized. Your desire is not something you labor to fulfill, it is recognizing something you already possess. It is assuming the feeling of being that which you desire to be.

Believing and being are one. The conceiver and his conception are one, therefore that which you conceive yourself to be can never be so far off as even to be near, for nearness implies separation.

*"If thou canst believe,
all things are possible to him that believeth."*

Being is the substance of things hoped for, the evidence of things not yet seen.

If you assume that you are what you want to be, then you will see others as they are related to your assumption.

8.

The mystery to which Paul referred when he wrote,

"This is a great mystery... He that loveth his wife loveth himself.... And they two shall be one flesh,"

is simply the mystery of consciousness.

Consciousness is really one and undivided but for creation's sake it appears to be divided into two.

The conscious (objective) or male aspect truly is the head and dominates the subconscious (subjective) or female aspect. However, this leadership is not that of the tyrant, but of the lover. So, by assuming the feeling that would be yours were you already in possession of your objective, the subconscious is moved to build the exact likeness of your assumption.

Your desires are not subconsciously accepted until you assume the feeling of their reality, for only through feeling is an idea subconsciously accepted and only through this subconscious acceptance is it ever expressed.

It is easier to ascribe your feeling to events in the world than to admit that the conditions of the world reflect your feeling. However, it is eternally true that the outside mirrors the inside.

9.

Prayer is the key which unlocks the infinite storehouse.

"Prove me now herewith, saith the Lord of hosts, if I will not open you the windows of heaven, and pour you out a blessing, that there shall not be room enough to receive it."

Prayer modifies or completely changes our subconscious assumptions, and a change of assumption is a change of expression.

The conscious mind reasons inductively from observation, experience and education. It therefore finds it difficult to believe what the five senses and inductive reason deny.

The subconscious reasons deductively and is never concerned with the truth or falsity of the premise, but proceeds on the assumption of the correctness of the premise and objectifies results which are consistent with the premise.

This distinction must be clearly seen by all who would master the art of praying.

No true grasp of the science of prayer can be really obtained until the laws governing the dual nature of consciousness are understood and the importance of the subconscious realized.

Prayer . . the art of believing what is denied by the senses . . deals almost entirely with the subconscious. Through prayer, the subconscious is suggested, into acceptance of the wish fulfilled, and, reasoning deductively, logically unfolds it to its legitimate end.

> *"Far greater is He that is in you*
> *than he that is in the world."*

10.

All transformation is based upon suggestion, and this can work only where you lay yourself completely open to an influence.

You must abandon yourself to your ideal as a woman abandons herself to love, for complete abandonment of self to it is the way to union with your ideal.

You must assume the feeling of the wish fulfilled until your assumption has all the sensory vividness of reality. You must imagine that you are already experiencing what you desire. That is, you must assume the feeling of the fulfillment of your desire until you are possessed by it and this feeling crowds all other ideas out of your consciousness.

The man who is not prepared for the conscious plunge into the assumption of the wish fulfilled in the faith that it is the only way to the realization of his dream is not yet ready to live consciously by the law of assumption, although there is no doubt that he does live by the law of assumption unconsciously.

But for you, who accept this principle and are ready to live by consciously assuming that your wish is already fulfilled, the adventure of life begins.

11.

The spiritual man speaks to the natural man through the language of desire. The key to progress in life and to the fulfillment of dreams lies in ready obedience to its voice. Unhesitating obedience to its voice is an immediate assumption of the wish fulfilled. To desire a state is to have it.

As Pascal has said,

"You would not have sought me
had you not already found me."

Man, by assuming the feeling of his wish fulfilled, and then living and acting on this conviction, alters the future in harmony with his assumption.

Assumptions awaken what they affirm. As soon as man assumes the feeling of his wish fulfilled, his four-dimensional self finds ways for the attainment of this end, discovers methods for its realization.

12.

The question is often asked,

"What should be done between the assumption of the wish fulfilled and its realization?"

Nothing.

It is a delusion that, other than assuming the feeling of the wish fulfilled, you can do anything to aid the realization of your desire.

You think that you can do something, you want to do something; but actually you can do nothing.

The illusion of the free will to do, is but ignorance of the law of assumption, upon which all action is based.

Everything happens automatically.

All that befalls you, all that is done by you . . happens.

Your assumptions, conscious or unconscious, direct all thought and action to their fulfillment.

To understand the law of assumption, to be convinced of its truth, means getting rid of all the illusions about free will to act.

Free will actually means freedom to select any idea you desire.

By assuming the idea already to be a fact, it is converted into reality. Beyond that, free will ends, and everything happens in harmony with the concept assumed.

13.

A change of fortune is a new direction and outlook, merely a change in arrangement of the same mind substance .. consciousness.

If you would change your life, you must begin at the very source with your own basic concept of self.

Outer change, becoming part of organizations, political bodies, religious bodies, is not enough. The cause goes deeper. The essential change must take place in yourself, in your own concept of self.

You must assume that you are what you want to be and continue therein, for the reality of your assumption has its being, in complete independence of objective fact and will clothe itself in flesh if you persist in the feeling of the wish fulfilled.

When you know that assumptions, if persisted in, harden into facts, then events which seem to the uninitiated mere accidents will be understood by you to be the logical and inevitable effects of your assumption.

The important thing to bear in mind is that you have infinite free will in choosing your assumptions, but no power to determine conditions and events.

You can create nothing, but your assumption determines what portion of creation you will experience.

14.

"Let the weak man say, 'I AM strong'",

for by his assumption, the cause-substance . . I AM . . is rearranged and must, therefore, manifest that which its rearrangement affirms. This principle governs every aspect of your life, be it social, financial, intellectual, or spiritual.

I AM is that reality to which, whatever happens, we must turn for an explanation of the phenomena of life. It is I AM's concept of itself that determines the form and scenery of its existence.

Everything depends upon its attitude towards itself; that which it will not affirm as true of itself cannot awaken in its world.

15.

"Not by might, nor by power, but by my spirit, saith the Lord of hosts."

Get into the spirit of the state desired by assuming the feeling that would be yours were you already the one you want to be. As you capture the feeling of the state sought, you are relieved of all effort to make it so, for it is already so.

There is a definite feeling associated with every idea in the mind of man.

Capture the feeling associated with your realized wish by assuming the feeling that would be yours were you already in possession of the thing you desire, and your wish will objectify itself.

Faith is feeling,

"According to your faith (feeling) be it unto you."

You never attract that which you want but always that which you are. As a man is, so does he see.

*"To him that hath it shall be given
and
to him that hath not it shall be taken away..."*

That which you feel yourself to be you are, and you are given that which you are. So assume the feeling that would be yours were you already in possession of your wish, and your wish must be realized.

16.

"Choose ye this day whom ye shall serve"

is your freedom to choose the kind of mood you assume; but the expression of the mood is the secret of the subconscious.

The subconscious receives impressions only through the feelings of man and, in a way known only to itself, gives these impressions form and expression.

The actions of man are determined by his subconscious impressions. His illusion of free will, his belief in freedom of action, is but ignorance of the causes which make him act.

He thinks himself free because he has forgotten the link between himself and the event.

Man awake is under compulsion to express his subconscious impressions. If in the past he unwisely impressed himself, then let him begin to change his thought and feeling, for only as he does so will he change his world.

Assume the feeling of the wish fulfilled.

17.

When William Blake wrote,

What seems to be, is, to those to whom it
seems to be,

he was only repeating the eternal truth,

there is nothing unclean of itself; but to
him that esteemeth anything to be unclean,
to him it is unclean.

Because there is nothing unclean of itself (or clean of itself), you should assume the best and think only of that which is lovely and of good report.

It is not superior insight, but ignorance of this law of assumption, if you read into the greatness of men some littleness with which you may be familiar . . or into some situation or circumstance an unfavorable conviction.

Your particular relationship to another influences your assumption with respect to that other and makes you see in him that which you do see. If you can change your opinion of another, then what you now believe of him cannot be absolutely true but is only relatively true.

18.

Your mood prior to sleep defines your state of consciousness as you enter into the presence of your everlasting lover, the subconscious. She sees you exactly as you feel yourself to be. If, as you prepare for sleep, you assume and maintain the consciousness of success by feeling

"I AM successful",

you must be successful.

19.

The changes which take place in your life as a result of your changed concept of yourself always appear to the unenlightened to be the result, not of a change of your consciousness, but of chance, outer cause, or coincidence.

However, the only fate governing your life is the fate determined by your own concepts, your own assumptions; for an assumption, though false, if persisted in, will harden into fact.

The ideal you seek and hope to attain will not manifest itself, will not be realized by you until you have imagined that you are already that ideal.

There is no escape for you except by a radical psychological transformation of yourself, except by your assumption of the feeling of your wish fulfilled. Therefore, make results or accomplishments the crucial test of your ability to use your imagination.

Everything depends on your attitude towards yourself. That which you will not affirm as true of yourself can never be realized by you, for that attitude alone is the necessary condition by which you realize your goal.

20.

Prayer is the art of assuming the feeling of being and having that which you want. When the senses confirm the absence of your wish, all conscious effort to counteract this suggestion is futile and tends to intensify the suggestion.

Prayer is the art of yielding to the wish and not the forcing of the wish. Whenever your feeling is in conflict with your wish, feeling will be the victor.

The dominant feeling invariably expresses itself. Prayer must be without effort. In attempting to fix an attitude of mind which is denied by the senses, effort is fatal.

21.

The following is an actual case history llustrating how the law of assumption works:

One day, a costume designer described to me her difficulties in working with a prominent theatrical producer. She was convinced that he unjustly criticized and rejected her best work and that often he was deliberately rude and unfair to her. Upon hearing her story, I explained that if she found the other rude and unfair, it was a sure sign that she, herself, was wanting and that it was not the producer, but herself that was in need of a new attitude.

I told her that the power of this law of assumption and its practical application could be discovered only through experience, and that only by assuming that the situation was already what she wanted it to be could she prove that she could bring about the change desired.

Her employer was merely bearing witness, telling her by his behavior what her concept of him was. I suggested that it was quite probable that she was carrying on conversations with him in her mind which were filled with criticism and recriminations.

There was no doubt but that she was mentally arguing with the producer, for others only echo that which we whisper to them in secret. I asked her if it was not true that she talked to him mentally, and, if so, what those conversations were like.

She confessed that every morning on her way to the theatre she told him just what she thought of him in a way she would never have dared address him in person. The intensity and force of her mental arguments with him automatically established his behavior towards her.

She began to realize that all of us carry on mental conversations, but, unfortunately, on most occasions, these conversations are argumentative... that we have only to observe the passerby on the street to prove this assertion... that so many people are mentally engrossed in conversation and few appear to be happy about it, but the very intensity of their feeling must lead them quickly to the unpleasant incident they themselves have mentally created and therefore must now encounter.

When she realized what she had been doing, she agreed to change her attitude and to live this law faithfully by assuming that her job was highly satisfactory and her relationship with the producer was a very happy one. To do this, she agreed that, before going to sleep at night, on her way to work, and at other intervals during the day, she would imagine that he had congratulated her on her fine designs and that she, in turn, had thanked him for his praise and kindness. To her great delight, she soon discovered for herself that her own attitude was the cause of all that befell her.

The behavior of her employer miraculously reversed itself. His attitude, echoing as it had always done, that which she had assumed, now reflected her changed concept of him.

What she did was by the power of her imagination. Her persistent assumption influenced his behavior and determined his attitude toward her.

> With the passport of desire on the wings
> of a controlled imagination, she traveled into the
> future of her own predetermined experience.

Thus we see it is not facts, but that which we create in our imagination, which shapes our lives, for most of the conflicts of the day are due to the want of a little imagination to cast the beam out of our own eye.

It is the exact and literal-minded who live in a fictitious world.

As this designer, by her controlled imagination, started the subtle change in her employer's mind, so can we, by the control of our own imagination and wisely directed feeling, solve our problems.

By the intensity of her imagination and feeling, the designer cast a kind of enchantment on her producer's mind and caused him to think that his generous praise originated with him. Often our most elaborate and original thoughts are determined by another.

> We should never be certain that it was
> not some woman treading in the winepress
> who began that subtle change in men's mind,
> or that the passion did not begin in the mind
> of some shepherd boy, lighting up his eyes
> for a moment before it ran upon its way.
> . . . William Butler Yeats

22.

"Man ought always to pray and not to faint."

Here, to pray means to give thanks for already having what you desire.

Only persistency in the assumption of the wish fulfilled can cause those subtle changes in your mind which result in the desired change in your life. It matters not whether they be "Angels", "Elisha", or "reluctant judges"; all must respond in harmony with your persistent assumption.

When it appears that people other than yourself in your world do not act toward you as you would like, it is not due to reluctance on their part, but a lack of persistence in your assumption of your life already being as you want it to be.

Your assumption, to be effective, cannot be a single isolated act; it must be a maintained attitude of the wish fulfilled.

And that maintained attitude that gets you there, so that you think from your wish fulfilled instead of thinking about your wish, is aided by assuming the feeling of the wish fulfilled frequently.

It is the frequency, not the length of time, that makes it natural. That to which you constantly return constitutes your truest self.

Frequent occupancy of the feeling of the wish fulfilled is the secret of success.

23.

All objective (visible) states were first subjective (invisible) states, and you called them into visible by assuming the feeling of their reality. The creative process is first imagining and then believing the state imagined. Always imagine and expect the best.

The world cannot change until you change your conception of it.

"As within, so without"

Nations, as well as people, are only what you believe them to be. No matter what the problem is, no matter where it is, no matter whom it concerns, you have no one to change but yourself, and you have neither opponent nor helper in bringing about the change within yourself.

You have nothing to do but convince yourself of the truth of that which you desire to see manifested. As soon as you succeed in convincing yourself of the reality of the state sought, results follow to confirm your fixed belief.

You never suggest to another the state which you desire to see him express; instead, you convince yourself that he is already that which you desire him to be.

Realization of your wish is accomplished by assuming the feeling of the wish fulfilled. You cannot fail unless you fail to convince yourself of the reality of your wish.

24.

Within that blankness we call sleep there is a consciousness in unsleeping vigilance, and while the body sleeps this unsleeping being releases from the treasure house of eternity the subconscious assumptions of man.

25.

Let us assume the feeling

"I AM Christ,"

and our whole behavior will subtly and unconsciously change in accordance with the assumption. Our subconscious assumptions continually externalize themselves that others may consciously see us as we subconsciously see ourselves, and tell us by their actions what we have subconsciously assumed of ourselves to be. Therefore let us assume the feeling

"I AM Christ,"

until our conscious claim becomes our subconscious assumption that

"We all with open face beholding as in a glass the glory of the Lord are changed into the same image from glory to glory."

Let God Awake and his enemies be destroyed. There is no greater prayer for man.

26.

Experience in imagination, with all the distinctness of reality, what would be experienced in the flesh were you to achieve your goal; and you shall, in time, meet it in the flesh as you met it in your imagination.

Feed the mind with premises, that is, assertions presumed to be true, because assumptions, though unreal to the senses, if persisted in, until they have the feeling of reality, will harden into facts.

To an assumption, all means which promote its realization, are good. It influences the behavior of all by inspiring in all the movements, the actions, and the words which tend towards its fulfillment.

27.

To reach a higher level of being, you must assume a higher concept of yourself. If you will not imagine yourself as other than what you are, then you remain as you are,

> *"for if ye believe not that I AM He,*
> *ye shall die in your sins."*

If you do not believe that you are He, the person you want to be, then you remain as you are.

Through the faithful systematic cultivation of the feeling of the wish fulfilled, desire becomes the promise of its own fulfillment.

The assumption of the feeling of the wish fulfilled makes the future dream a present fact.

28.

Assume that you are that which you want to be. Experience in imagination what you would experience in the flesh were you already that which you want to be. Remain faithful to your assumption, so that you define yourself as that which you have assumed.

Things have no life if they are severed from their roots, and our consciousness, our "I AMness," is the root of all that springs in our world.

"If ye believe not that I am he, ye shall die in your sins".

That is, if I do not believe that I am already that which I desire to be, then I remain as I am and die in my present concept of self.

There is no power, outside of the consciousness of man, to resurrect and make alive that which man desires to experience.

That man who is accustomed to call up at will, whatever images he pleases, will be, by virtue of the power of his imagination, master of his fate.

*"I AM the resurrection, and the life:
he that believeth in me,
though he were dead, yet shall he live."*

*"Ye shall know the truth,
and the truth shall make you free."*

29.

The unconsciousness of sleep is the normal state of the subconscious. Because all things come from within yourself, and your conception of yourself determines that which comes, you should always feel the wish fulfilled before you drop off to sleep. You never draw out of the deep of yourself that which you want; you always draw that which you are, and you are that which you feel yourself to be as well as that which you feel as true of others.

To be realized, then, the wish must be resolved into the feeling of being or having or witnessing the state sought. This is accomplished by assuming the feeling of the wish fulfilled. The feeling which comes in response to the question

"How would I feel were my wish realized?"

is the feeling which should monopolize and immobilize your attention as you relax into sleep. You must be in the consciousness of being or having that which you want to be or to have before you drop off to sleep.

Once asleep, man has no freedom of choice. His entire slumber is dominated by his last waking concept of self. It follows, therefore, that he should always assume the feeling of accomplishment and satisfaction before he retires in sleep,

30.

The drama of life is a psychological one, in which all the conditions, circumstances and events of your life are brought to pass by your assumptions.

Since your life is determined by your assumptions, you are forced to recognize the fact that you are either a slave to your assumptions or their master. To become the master of your assumptions is the key to undreamed of freedom and happiness.

You can attain this mastery by deliberate conscious control of your imagination.

You determine your assumptions in this way:

Form a mental image, a picture of the state desired, of the person you want to be. Concentrate your attention upon the feeling that you are already that person. First, visualize the picture in your consciousness. Then feel yourself to be in that state as though it actually formed your surrounding world.

By your imagination that which was a mere mental image is changed into a seemingly solid reality.

The great secret is a controlled imagination and a well sustained attention firmly and repeatedly focused on the object to be accomplished. It cannot be emphasized too much that, by creating an ideal within your mental sphere, by assuming that you are already that ideal, you identify yourself with it and thereby transform yourself into its image, thinking from the ideal instead of thinking of the ideal.

Every state is already there as "mere possibilities" as long as we think of them, but as overpoweringly real when we think from them.

This was called by the ancient teachers

"Subjection to the will of God"

or

"Resting in the Lord",

and the only true test of "Resting in the Lord" is that all who do rest are inevitably transformed into the image of that in which they rest, thinking from the wish fulfilled.

You become according to your resigned will, and your resigned will is your concept of yourself and all that you consent to and accept as true. You, assuming the feeling of your wish fulfilled and continuing therein, take upon yourself the results of that state; not assuming the feeling of your wish fulfilled, you are ever free of the results.

31.

The ancient teachers warned us not to judge from appearances because, said they, the truth need not conform to the external reality to which it relates.

They claimed that we bore false witness if we imagined evil against another, that no matter how real our belief appears to be, how truly it conforms to the external reality to which it relates, if it does not make free, the one of whom we hold the belief, it is untrue and therefore a false judgment.

We are called upon to deny the evidence of our senses and to imagine as true of our neighbor that which makes him free.

"Ye shall know the truth, and the truth shall make you free."

To know the truth of our neighbor we must assume that he is already that which he desires to be. Any concept we hold of another that is short of his fulfilled desire, will not make him free and therefore cannot be the truth.

32.

Look as though you saw, listen as though you heard; stretch forth your imaginary hand as though you touched .. and your assumptions will harden into facts.

33.

Night after night, you should assume the feeling of being, having and witnessing that which you seek to be, possess and see manifested.

Never go to sleep feeling discouraged or dissatisfied.

Never sleep in the consciousness of failure.

Your subconscious, whose natural state is sleep, sees you as you believe yourself to be, and whether it be good, bad or indifferent, the subconscious will faithfully embody your belief.

As you feel, so do you impress her; and she, the perfect lover, gives form to these impressions and out pictures them as the children of her beloved.

"Thou art all fair, my love; there is no spot in thee,"

is the attitude of mind to adopt before dropping off to sleep. Disregard appearances and feel that things are as you wish them to be, for

> "He calleth things that are not seen as though they were, and the unseen becomes seen."

To assume the feeling of satisfaction is to call conditions into being which will mirror satisfaction.

"Signs follow, they do not precede".

Proof that you are will follow the consciousness that you are; it will not precede it.

You are an eternal dreamer dreaming non-eternal dreams. Your dreams take form as you assume the feeling of their reality. Do not limit yourself to the past. Knowing that nothing is impossible to consciousness, begin to imagine states beyond the experiences of the past.

Whatever the mind of man can imagine, man can realize.

34.

Experiments recently conducted by Merle Lawrence (Princeton) and Adelbert Ames (Dartmouth) in the latter's psychology laboratory at Hanover, N.H., prove that what you see when you look at something depends not so much on what is there as on the assumption you make when you look.

Since what we believe to be the "real" physical world is actually only an "assumptive" world, it is not surprising that these experiments prove that what appears to be solid reality is actually the result of "expectations" or "assumptions".

Your assumptions determine not only what you see, but also what you do, for they govern all your conscious and subconscious movements towards the fulfillment of themselves.

35.

All is yours.

Do not go seeking for that which you are.

Appropriate it, claim it, assume it.

Everything depends upon your concept of yourself. That which you do not claim as true of yourself cannot be realized by you. The promise is,

> *"Whosoever hath, to him it shall be given, and he shall have more abundance; but whosoever hath not, from him shall be taken away even that which he seemeth to have."*

Hold fast, in your imagination, to all that is lovely and of good report, for the lovely and the good are essential in your life if it is to be worthwhile. Assume it. You do this by imagining that you already are what you want to be and already have what you want to have.

> *"As a man thinketh in his heart, so is he."*

Be still and know that you are that which you desire to be, and you will never have to search for it.

In spite of your appearance of freedom of action, you obey, as everything else does, the law of assumption. Whatever you may think of the question of free will, the truth is your experiences throughout your life are determined by your assumptions . . whether conscious or unconscious.

> An assumption builds a bridge of incidents that lead inevitably to the fulfillment of itself.

Man believes the future to be the natural development of the past. But the law of assumption clearly shows that this is not the case. Your assumption places you psychologically where you are not physically; then your senses pull you back from where you were psychologically to where you are physically. It is these psychological forward motions that produce your physical forward motions in time. Precognition permeates all the scriptures of the world.

36.

All transformation begins with an intense, burning desire to be transformed. The first step in the

"renewing of the mind"

is desire. You must want to be different, and intend to be, before you can begin to change yourself. Then you must make your future dream a present fact.

You do this by assuming the feeling of your wish fulfilled. By desiring to be other than what you are, you can create an ideal of the person you want to be and assume that you are already that person. If this assumption is persisted in until it becomes your dominant feeling, the attainment of your ideal is inevitable.

37.

*"****Whatsoever things ye desire***, when ye pray believe that you have received them, and ye shall have them."*

The only condition required is that you believe that your prayers are already realized.

Your prayer must be answered if you assume the feeling that would be yours were you already in possession of your objective. The moment you accept the wish as an accomplished fact, the subconscious finds means for its realization.

To pray successfully then, you must yield to the wish, that is, feel the wish fulfilled.

The perfectly disciplined man is always in tune with the wish as an accomplished fact. He knows that consciousness is the one and only reality, that ideas and feelings are facts of consciousness and are as real as objects in space; therefore he never entertains a feeling which does not contribute to his happiness, for feelings are the causes of the actions and circumstances of his life.

38.

Over a century ago, this truth was stated by Emerson as follows:

> As the world was plastic and fluid in the
> hands of God, so it is ever to so much of
> his attributes as we bring to it. To ignorance
> and sin, it is flint. They adapt themselves to
> it as they may, but in proportion as a man has
> anything in him divine, the firmament flows
> before him and takes his signet and form.

Your assumption is the hand of God molding the firmament into the image of that which you assume. The assumption of the wish fulfilled is the high tide which lifts you easily off the bar of the senses where you have so long lain stranded. It lifts the mind into prophecy in the full right sense of the word; and if you have that controlled imagination and absorbed attention which it is possible to attain, you may be sure that all your assumption implies will come to pass.

39.

The principle of "Least Action" governs everything in physics, from the path of a planet to the path of a pulse of light.

Least Action is the minimum of energy, multiplied by the minimum of time. Therefore, in moving from your present state to the state desired, you must use the minimum of energy and take the shortest possible time.

Your journey from one state of consciousness to another is a psychological one, so, to make the journey, you must employ the psychological equivalent of "Least Action" and the psychological equivalent is mere assumption.

The day you fully realize the power of assumption, you discover that it works in complete conformity with this principle. It works by means of attention, minus effort. Thus, with least action, through an assumption, you hurry without haste and reach your goal without effort.

Because creation is finished, what you desire already exists.

It is excluded from view because you can see only the contents of your own consciousness. It is the function of an assumption to call back the excluded view and restore full vision.

It is not the world, but your assumptions that change. An assumption brings the invisible into sight. It is nothing more nor less than seeing with the eye of God, i.e., imagination.

> *"For the Lord seeth not as a man seeth,*
> *for man looketh on the outward appearance,*
> *but the Lord looketh on the heart."*

The heart is the primary organ of sense, hence the first cause of experience. When you look "on the heart", you are looking at your assumptions: assumptions determine your experience. Watch your assumption with all diligence, for out of it are the issues of life. Assumptions have the power of objective realization.

40.

The assumption of the wish fulfilled is the ship that carries you over the unknown seas to the fulfillment of your dream.

The assumption is everything; realization is subconscious and effortless.

> *"Assume a virtue if you have it not."*

Act on the assumption that you already possess that which you sought.

"Blessed is she that believed; for there shall be a performance of those things which were told her from the Lord."

As the Immaculate Conception is the foundation of the Christian mysteries, so the Assumption is their crown.

Psychologically, the Immaculate Conception means the birth of an idea in your own consciousness, unaided by another.

For instance, when you have a specific wish or hunger or longing, it is an immaculate conception in the sense that no physical person or thing plants it in your mind. It is self-conceived.

Every man is the Mary of the Immaculate Conception and birth to his idea must give. The Assumption is the crown of the mysteries because it is the highest use of consciousness. When in imagination you assume the feeling of the wish fulfilled, you are mentally lifted up to a higher level.

When, through your persistence, this assumption becomes actual fact, you automatically find yourself on a higher level, that is, you have achieved your desire, in your objective world.

Your assumption guides all your conscious and subconscious movements towards its suggested end so inevitably that it actually dictates the events.

The drama of life is a psychological one and the whole of it is written and produced by your assumptions.

Learn the art of assumption, for only in this way can you create your own happiness.

41.

Every moment of your life, consciously or unconsciously, you are assuming a feeling. You can no more avoid assuming a feeling than you can avoid eating and drinking.

All you can do is control the nature of your assumptions. Thus it is clearly seen that the control of your assumption is the key you now hold to an ever expanding, happier, more noble life.

42.

The outer, physical events of life are the fruit of forgotten blossom-times, results of previous and usually forgotten states of consciousness. They are the ends running true to oft-times forgotten imaginative origins.

Whenever you become completely absorbed in an emotional state, you are at that moment assuming the feeling of the state fulfilled.

If persisted in, whatsoever you are intensely emotional about, you will experience in your world. These periods of absorption, of concentrated attention, are the beginnings of the things you harvest.

It is in such moments that you are exercising your creative power, the only creative power there is.

43.

Remain faithful to the knowledge that your consciousness, your I AMness, your awareness of being aware of the only reality. It is the rock on which all phenomena can be explained.

There is no explanation outside of that. I know of no clear conception of the origin of phenomena save that consciousness is all and all is consciousness.

That which you seek is already housed within you. Were it not now within you eternity could not evolve it. No time stretch would be long enough to evolve what is not potentially involved in you.

You simply let it into being by assuming that it is already visible in your world, and remaining faithful to your assumption. it will harden into fact. Your Father has unnumbered ways of revealing your assumption. Fix this in your mind and always remember,

> "An assumption, though false, if sustained
> will harden into fact."

44.

Everything we do, unaccompanied by a change of consciousness, is but futile readjustment of surfaces. However we toil or struggle, we can receive no more than our assumptions affirm. To protest against anything which happens to us is to protest against the law of our being and our rulership over our own destiny.

45.

"Be ye doers of the word and not hearers only,
deceiving your own selves. For if any be a hearer

> *of the word, and not a doer, he is like unto a man beholding his natural face in a glass and goeth his way, and straightway forgetteth what manner of man he was. But whoso looketh into the perfect law of liberty, and continue therein, he being not a forgetful hearer but a doer of the work, this man shall be blessed in his deed."*

The word, in this quotation, means idea, concept, or desire.

You deceive yourself by "hearing only" when you expect your desire to be fulfilled through mere wishful thinking.

Your desire is what you want to be, and looking at yourself "in a glass" is seeing yourself in imagination as that person.

Forgetting "what manner of man" you are is failing to persist in your assumption.

The "perfect law of liberty" is the law which makes possible liberation from limitation, that is, the law of assumption. To continue in the perfect law of liberty is to persist in the assumption that your desire is already fulfilled.

You are not a "forgetful hearer" when you keep the feeling of your wish fulfilled constantly alive in your consciousness.

This makes you a "doer of the work", and you are blessed in your deed by the inevitable realization of your desire.

You must be doers of the law of assumption, for without application, the most profound understanding will not produce any desired result. Frequent reiteration and repetition of important basic truths runs through these pages.

Where the law of assumption is concerned . . the law that sets man free . . this is a good thing. It should be made clear again and again even at the risk of repetition. The real truth-seeker will welcome this aid in concentrating his attention upon the law which sets him free.

The parable of the Master's condemnation of the servant who neglected to use the talent given him is clear and unmistakable.

Having discovered within yourself the key to the Treasure House, you should be like the good servant who, by wise use, multiplied by many times the talents entrusted to him.

The talent entrusted to you is the power to consciously determine your assumption. The talent not used, like the limb not exercised, withers and finally atrophies.

What you must strive after is being. In order to do, it is necessary to be. The end of yearning is to be. Your concept of yourself can only be driven out of consciousness by another concept of yourself.

By creating an ideal in your mind, you can identify yourself with it until you become one and the same with the ideal, thereby transforming yourself into it.

The dynamic prevails over the static; the active over the passive. One who is a doer is magnetic and therefore infinitely more creative than any who merely hear.
Be among the doers.

46.

What is called creativeness is only becoming aware of what already is. You simply become aware of increasing portions of that which already exists.

The fact that you can never be anything that you are not already or experience anything not already existing explains the experience of having an acute feeling of having heard before what is being said, or having met before the person being met for the first time, or having seen before a place or thing being seen for the first time.

The whole of creation exists in you, and it is your destiny to become increasingly aware of its infinite wonders and to experience ever greater and grander portions of it.

If creation is finished, and all events are taking place now, the question that springs naturally to the mind is

"what determines your time track?"

That is, what determines the events which you encounter?

And the answer is your concept of yourself. Concepts determine the route that attention follows.

Here is a good test to prove this fact. Assume the feeling of your wish fulfilled and observe the route that your attention follows. You will observe that as long as you remain faithful to your assumption, so long will your attention be confronted with images clearly related to that assumption.
For example;

if you assume that you have a wonderful business, you will notice how in your imagination, your attention is focused on incident after incident relating to that assumption.

Friends congratulate you, tell you how lucky you are. Others are envious and critical. From there, your attention goes to larger offices, bigger bank balances, and many other similarly related events.

Persistence in this assumption will result in actually experiencing in fact that which you assumed.

The same is true regarding any concept. If your concept of yourself is that you are a failure, you would encounter in your imagination a whole series of incidents in conformance to that concept.

Thus it is clearly seen how you, by your concept of yourself, determine your present, that is, the particular portion of creation which you now experience, and your future, that is, the particular portion of creation which you will experience.

47.

And I say unto you, Ask, and it shall be given you;
seek, and ye shall find; knock, and it shall be opened unto you."

Ask, seek, and knock mean assuming the consciousness of already having what you desire.

Thus the scriptures tell you that you must persist in rising to (assuming) the consciousness of your wish already being fulfilled.

The promise is definite that if you are shameless in your impudence in assuming that you already have that which your senses deny, it shall be given unto you . . your desire shall be attained.

48.

It is of great significance that the truth of the principles outlined in this book have been proven time and again by the personal experiences of the Author.

Throughout the past twenty-five years, he has applied these principles and proved them successful in innumerable instances. He attributes to an unwavering assumption of his wish already being fulfilled every success that he has achieved.

He was confident that, by these fixed assumptions, his desires were predestined to be fulfilled. Time and again, he assumed the feeling of his wish fulfilled and continued in his assumption until that which he desired was completely realized.

Live your life in a sublime spirit of confidence and determination; disregard appearances, conditions, in fact all evidence of your senses that deny the fulfillment of your desire.

Rest in the assumption that you are already what you want to be, for, in that determined assumption, you and your Infinite Being are merged in creative unity, and with your Infinite Being (God) all things are possible. God never fails.

*"For who can stay His hand or say
unto Him, What doest thou?"*

Through the mastery of your assumptions, you are in very truth enabled to master life.

It is thus that the ladder of life is ascended: thus the ideal is realized.

The clue to the real purpose of life is to surrender yourself to your ideal with such awareness of its reality that you begin to live the life of the ideal and no longer your own life as it was prior to this surrender.

"He calleth things that are not seen as though they were, and the unseen becomes seen".

Each assumption has its corresponding world.

If you are truly observant, you will notice the power of your assumptions to change circumstances which appear wholly immutable.

You, by your conscious assumptions, determine the nature of the world in which you live.

Ignore the present state and assume the wish fulfilled.

Claim it; it will respond.

The law of assumption is the means by which the fulfillment of your desires may be realized.

49.

The ideal is always waiting to be incarnated, but unless we ourselves offer the ideal to the Lord, our consciousness, by assuming that we are already that which we seek to embody, it is incapable of birth.

The Lord needs his daily lamb of faith to mold the world in harmony with our dreams.

> *"By faith Abel offered unto God a*
> *More excellent sacrifice than Cain."*

Faith sacrifices the apparent fact for the unapparent truth.

Faith holds fast to the fundamental truth that through the medium of an assumption, invisible states become visible facts.

> *"For what is faith unless it is to*
> *believe what you do not see?"*
> *. . . St. Augustine*

50.

> **"A miracle is the name given, by those**
> *Who have no faith, to the works of faith.*
> *Faith is the substance of things hoped*
> *for, the evidence of things not seen."*

The very reason for the law of assumption is contained in this quotation.

If there were not a deep seated awareness that that which you hope for had substance and was possible of attainment, it would be impossible to assume the consciousness of being or having it.

It is the fact that creation is finished and everything exists that stirs you to hope, and hope, in turn, implies expectation, and without expectation of success, it would be impossible to use consciously the law of assumption.

"Evidence" is a sign of actuality.

Thus, this quotation means, that faith is the awareness of the reality of that which you assume, a conviction of the reality of things which you do not see, the mental perception of the reality of the invisible.

Consequently, it is obvious that a lack of faith means disbelief in the existence of that which you desire. Inasmuch as that which you experience is the faithful reproduction of your state of consciousness, lack of faith will mean perpetual failure in any conscious use of the law of assumption.

51.

If you want to build a magnet, you can do so only by conforming to the law of magnetism. In other words, you surrender yourself, or yield to the law. In like manner, when you use the faculty of assumption, you are conforming to a law just as real as the law governing magnetism.

You can neither create nor change the law of assumption.

It is in this respect that you are impotent. You can only yield or conform, and since all of your experiences are the result of your assumptions, consciously or unconsciously, the value of consciously using the power of assumption surely must be obvious.

Willingly identify yourself with that which you most desire, knowing that it will find expression through you.

Yield to the feeling of the wish fulfilled and be consumed as its victim, then rise as the prophet of the law of assumption.

52.

"I can of Mine Own Self do
nothing... because
I seek not Mine Own Will, but
the Will of the
Father which hath sent Me."

In this quotation, the Father obviously refers to God. In an earlier chapter, God is defined as I AM. Since creation is finished, the Father is never in a position of saying "I will be".

In other words, everything exists, and the infinite I AM consciousness can speak only in the present tense.

"Not My Will, but Thine be done."

"I will be" is a confession that "I AM not".

The Father's Will is always "I AM".

Until you realize that you are the Father (there is only one I AM, and your infinite self is that I AM), your will is always "I will be".

In the law of assumption, your consciousness of being is the Father's will. The mere wish without this consciousness is the "my will".

This great quotation, so little understood, is a perfect statement of the law of assumption.

It is impossible to do anything. You must be in order to do.

If you had a different concept of yourself, everything would be different. You are what you are, so everything is as it is. The events which you observe are determined by the concept you have of yourself. If you change your concept of yourself, the events ahead of you in time are altered, but, thus altered, they form again a deterministic sequence starting from the moment of this changed concept.

You are a being with powers of intervention, which enable you, by a change of consciousness, to alter the course of observed events, in fact, to change your future.

Deny the evidence of the senses, and assume the feeling of the wish fulfilled.

Inasmuch as your assumption is creative and forms an atmosphere, your assumption, if it be a noble one, increases your assurance and helps you to reach a higher level of being.

If, on the other hand, your assumption be an unlovely one, it hinders you and makes your downward way swifter. Just as the lovely assumptions create a harmonious atmosphere, so the hard and bitter feelings create a hard and bitter atmosphere.

> "Whatsoever things are pure, just, lovely,
> of good report, think on these things."

This means to make your assumptions the highest, noblest, happiest concepts. There is no better time to start than now. The present moment is always the most opportune in which to eliminate all unlovely assumptions and to concentrate only on the good.

As well as yourself, claim for others their Divine inheritance. See only their good and the good in them. Stir the highest in others to confidence and self-assertion by your sincere assumption of their good, and you will be their prophet and their healer, for an inevitable fulfillment awaits all sustained assumptions.

You win by assumption what you can never win by force.

An assumption is a certain motion of consciousness. This motion, like all motion, exercises an influence on the surrounding substance causing it to take the shape of, echo, and reflect the assumption.

53.

*"**Prove Me now herewith, saith the Lord** of hosts, if I will not open you the windows of heaven, and pour you out a blessing, that there shall not be room enough to receive it."*

The windows of heaven may not be opened and the treasures seized by a strong will, but they open of themselves and present their treasures as a free gift, a gift that comes when absorption reaches such a degree that it results in a feeling of complete acceptance.

The passage from your present state to the feeling of your wish fulfilled is not across a gap. There is continuity between the so-called real and unreal.

To cross from one state to the other, you simply extend your feelers, trust your touch and enter fully into the spirit of what you are doing.

> "Not by might nor by power, but by My Spirit, saith the Lord of hosts."

Assume the spirit, the feeling of the wish fulfilled, and you will have opened the windows to receive the blessing.

To assume a state is to get into the spirit of it. Your triumphs will be a surprise only to those who did not know your hidden passage from the state of longing to the assumption of the wish fulfilled.

The Lord of hosts will not respond to your wish until you have assumed the feeling of already being what you want to be, for acceptance is the channel of His action.

Acceptance is the Lord of hosts in action.

54.

I am not advocating philosophical indifference when I suggest that we should imagine ourselves as already that which we want to be, living in a mental atmosphere of greatness, rather than using physical means and arguments to bring about the desired change.

Everything we do, unaccompanied by a change of consciousness, is but futile readjustment of surfaces. However we toil or struggle, we can receive no more than our subconscious assumptions affirm.

To protest against anything which happens to us is to protest against the law of our being and our rulership over our own destiny.

The circumstances of my life are too closely related to my conception of myself not to have been launched by my own spirit from some magical storehouse of my being. If there is pain to me in these happenings, I should rook within myself for the cause, for I am moved here and there and made to live in a world in harmony with my concept of myself.

55.

The man who at will can assume whatever state he pleases has found the keys to the Kingdom of Heaven.

The keys are desire, imagination, and a steadily focused attention on the feeling of the wish fulfilled.

To such a man, any undesirable objective fact is no longer a reality and the ardent wish no longer a dream.

56.

The ideas and moods to which you constantly return define the state with which you are fused. Therefore train yourself to occupy more frequently the feeling of your wish fulfilled. This is creative magic. It is the way to work toward fusion with the desired state.

If you would assume the feeling of your wish fulfilled more frequently, you would be master of your fate, but unfortunately you shut out your assumption for all but the occasional hour. Practice making real to yourself the feeling of the wish fulfilled.

After you have assumed the feeling of the wish fulfilled, do not close the experience as you would a book, but carry it around like a fragrant odor.

Instead of being completely forgotten, let it remain in the atmosphere communicating its influence automatically to your actions and reactions. A mood, often repeated, gains a momentum that is hard to break or check. So be careful of the feelings you entertain. Habitual moods reveal the state with which you are fused.

57.

Suppose I am capable of acting with continuous imagination, that is, suppose I am capable of sustaining the feeling of my wish fulfilled, will my assumption harden into fact?

And, if it does harden into fact, shall I on reflection find that my actions through the period of incubation have been reasonable? Is my imagination a power sufficient, not merely to assume the feeling of the wish fulfilled, but is it also of itself capable of incarnating the idea?

After assuming that I am already what I want to be, must I continually guide myself by reasonable ideas and actions in order to bring about the fulfillment of my assumption?

Experience has convinced me that an assumption, though false, if persisted in, will harden into fact, that continuous imagination is sufficient for all things, and all my reasonable plans and actions will never make up for my lack of continuous imagination.

58.

As already stated, righteousness is the consciousness of already being what you want to be.

> *"By faith he forsook Egypt, not fearing the wrath of the king: for he endured, as seeing Him Who is invisible."*

"Egypt" means darkness, belief in many gods (causes).

The "king" symbolizes the power of outside conditions or circumstances.

"He" is your concept of yourself as already being what you want to be.

"Enduring as seeing Him Who is invisible"

means persisting in the assumption that your desire is already fulfilled.

Thus, this quotation means that, by persisting in the assumption that you already are the person you want to be, you rise above all doubt, fear, and belief in the power of outside conditions or circumstances; and your world inevitably conforms to your assumption.

59.

I tell you: imagination will not fail you if you are faithful. What could I say when I was confronted with the negation of my assumption? Nothing. I simply would not give up, and when the time was right my assumption became a fact. I urge you to set your goal high. Assume the feeling it has been reached and sleep in that feeling.

Persist and I promise you that not one thing in this world can rob you of that which you have assumed. But the most important thing is to know that which is housed within you is God's plan of redemption, and he only redeems himself. God came down into the world and housed himself in you. Now he is going to discover who he is, for it is in you as a person that the nature of God is revealed.

60.

Take his wonderful precept and believe that you can have anything you desire. There is no restriction placed upon the power of belief. There is no need to first consult some holy man to see whether you should have it or not. You be the judge. Choose your desire and, to the degree that you are self-persuaded that you have it, you will get it. And, because we are all one, if it takes one million people to aid the birth of your assumption, they will do it, without their knowledge or consent, so you don't have to ask anyone to aid you. They will do it not even knowing that they are. All you are called upon to do is to assume that you have it. An assumption, though false, if persisted in will harden into fact. That is the principle.

61.

Assume your wish through the sense of feeling. That assumption, subjectively appropriated and believed to be true, is faith. Can you believe in its reality? Knowing all things are possible to him who believes, can you persuade yourself that, although your reason and senses deny it, your assumption will make it so? Blake, in his wonderful "Marriage of Heaven and Hell," said: "I dined with Isaiah and Ezekiel and asked: Does a strong persuasion that a thing is so, make it so? and Isaiah replied: All prophets believe it does, and in ages of imagination a firm persuasion moved mountains, but many today are not capable of a firm persuasion of anything." Everything here was once only a desire, believed. This building, the clothes you wear or the car you drive were first a desire, then believed into being.

Yes, I believe there is a man named Neville. He may work for you to aid the fulfillment of your desire, if you believe you have it. Many men can and will come to aid you, even without knowing they are doing it, if you believe. You do not have to persuade others to help you; all you need do is believe you are what you want to be and then let the world (which is nothing more than yourself pushed out) go to work to make your assumption possible. I promise you: your desire will be fulfilled, for all things are possible to him who believes.

62.

To change your present state you, like Dr. Millikan, must rise to a higher level of consciousness. This rise is accomplished by affirming that you already are what you want to be, and assuming the feeling of your fulfilled desire.

The drama of life is a psychological one, brought about by your attitudes rather than by your acts. There is no escape from your present predicament other than a radical psychological transformation. Everything depends upon your attitude towards yourself, as that which you will not affirm as true of yourself, will not develop in your life.

The meek men of the gospels are not the proverbial poor, groveling door mats, as a meek man is generally conceived to be, but the Dr. Millikan's of the world who, while poor and unproven, dare to assume wealth and greatness.

These are the men who inherit the earth. Any concept of self less than the best robs you, and the promise is, "Blessed are the meek, for they shall inherit the earth."

63.

To say: "I AM going to be rich," will not make it happen; you must believe riches in by claiming within yourself: "I AM rich." You must believe in the present tense, because the active, creative power that you are, is God. He is your awareness, and God alone acts and is. His name forever and ever is "I AM" therefore, he can't say: "I will be rich" or "I was rich" but "I AM rich!" Claim what you want to be aware of here and now, and . . although your reasonable mind denies it and your senses deny it . . if you will assume it, with feeling, your inward activity, established and perpetuated, will objectify itself in the outside world . . which is nothing more than your imaginal activity, objectified. To attempt to change the circumstances of your life before you change its imaginal activity, is to labor in vain.

64.

A true judgment need not conform to the external facts to which it relates. Truth depends upon the intensity of imagining and not upon facts. So, I will imagine that I AM _____ and I name it, that which I want to be, and believing that I AM that which I AM assuming I AM and remaining loyal to the assumption, I become it. I have done it.

65.

Now, the virgin birth . . can I bring it from its invisible state and really make it a tangible fact within my world? Try it! As you try it with one thing and you succeed, you will try it with two and four and eight and so on, and eventually the sleeping giant in man . . which is the Son of God in man called Christ . . will awaken. He will awaken by moving from the passive state to the active state. The passive state is simply the complete and utter surrender of man to appearances, to live believing that life is on the outside, and he moves from that state where he surrenders and believes all these things to be causes to the active state, where he puts everything in subjection to that something within himself which is his awakened imagination. He imagines a thing to be so; he persuades himself that it is so and walks faithful to his assumption.

66.

The world was constructed in the mind's eye, out of things unseen by the mortal eye, and made alive by faith. Eternity exists and all things in eternity, independent of the creative act, which is the assumption of unseen reality and loyalty to its assemblage.

In spite of denial by your senses and reason, if you will be faithful to your unseen assumption, it will externalize itself. That is how all worlds come into being, but men do not understand this. Structuring their world based upon the evidence of their senses, they continue to perpetuate that which they do not desire.

Knowing what you want, close your eyes and enter its fulfillment, knowing that God is seeing what you are seeing. That He is hearing what you are saying; and what God sees and hears and remains loyal to, He externalizes.

67.

There is no limit to your creative power. The most horrible problem will be resolved if you will but conceive a solution in your mind's eye. Anyone can do it. It doesn't take an Einstein to imagine a problem is resolved. Do not limit your creative power by determining the ways and means for it to come about, for imagination has at its disposal ways that are past finding out.

Do not be concerned as to how, when, or where . . only the end. If you are in debt, what is the solution? That you win the lottery or an uncle dies and leaves you his fortune?

No! The end is that you are debt-free. How would you feel if all of your bills were paid? Assume that feeling and let imagination harden that feeling into a fact!

Every problem has a solution. Imagine the solution and assume it is true. What would you see and do were it true? How would you feel? Persist in that feeling and in a way no one knows the solution will come to pass.

68.

If you can imagine the end, knowing all things are possible to imagination and remain faithful to that assumption as though it were true, imagination will harden into fact. Remember, creative power will not operate itself. Knowing what to do is not enough. You, imagination's operant power, must be willing to assume that things are as you desire them to be before they can ever come to pass.

69.

I am told, as you are told tonight, that it is possible that I can assume I am the man I would like to be. If I dare to remain faithful to that assumption and not waver in it . . and to the degree that I am loyal to that assumption . . it will crystallize and become a fact. I need not appeal to any person in the world to help me. I can do it all by myself if I know of the existence of the Being in me who is skilled in arranging things so that it leads to a desired end. How would I arrange the furniture of the mind to reach the desired end, but name the end first . . the end is where I begin. My end is my beginning.

70.

While we are here, we can use the Law that was given us. It's a simple law, and it will not fail you. But you must believe in Him. And you cannot believe in the Lord Jesus Christ, believing in someone other than your own wonderful human imagination . . not the real Lord Jesus Christ. If you want results, believe in the true Jesus, and the true Jesus is your imagination. And all things are possible to the human imagination, therefore, all things are possible to Jesus Christ, So, imagine yourself (and you name it).

Believe in the reality of what you imagine. Persist in that assumption, and that assumption, though at the moment that you made it, it is denied by your senses, if you persist in it, it will become a fact. It will actually harden into some objective state.

71.

There is only one God and Father of us all who is above all, through all, and in all. If He is in every being who says I AM, and there is only one God, no one can accuse another; for God's name is not he is, but I AM. No matter what appears on the outside, I AM its cause. Assume full responsibility for the things you observe, and if you do not like what you see, know you have the power to change them. Then exercise that power and you will observe the change you caused. If you are truly willing to assume that responsibility, you are set free.

72.

You can't just say, I would like to be it; you must assume that you are it, and sleep in the assumption that you are it, for the assumption, though at the moment denied by your senses . . denied by everything round about you, if persisted in will harden into fact. So, you dare to assume that you are the man . . the woman . . that you want to be, and day after day live in that assumption as though it were true, and that assumption will become a reality in the world. Even if you go hungry, it doesn't matter. No matter what happens, go hungry; but persist in the assumption, and that assumption will objectify itself and become a reality in your world.

73.

Don't neglect the law of God which is: An assumption will harden into fact. If an assumption creates its own reality then there is no such thing as fiction. I may forget what I assumed today and when it appears I may not recognize my own harvest, but it could not enter my world had I not brought it in by an imaginal act.

74.

You can play any part . . be it a rich man or a poor man, a beggar or a thief, the known or unknown . . once you know they are only parts, only states of consciousness. But if you don't know this, and are not willing to give up your present state, you will remain there, looking at your desire and not from it. You can become what you would like to be in the twinkle of an eye by the simple act of assumption.

And the day you dare to remain faithful to your assumption, it will begin to externalize itself. And when it does you may return to sleep, just as you do in your night dreams. Becoming possessed by the dream you created in your sleep, you observe your own creation; and if it is a noble dream, you can become so puffed up in your own concept that you forget its creator. Or you can create something ignoble and become so immersed in it you believe in its reality. Anything can be created by a mere assumption. When I dared to assume I was the man I wanted to be, I did not discuss it with others; I simply persisted in my assumption and watched it harden into fact. That persistent act taught me that this world was a dream.

75.

Do you like what the mirror reflects back to you and your background tells you? If it is not what you would like to live with, don't accept it. Rather, look into the mirror of your mind and assume that you are what you would like to be. Declaring that you are now it, don't look away and forget the image reflected there, but persist in your assumption. Live in that awareness morning, noon and night as though it were true, and no power can stop you from experiencing its truth.

76.

Dare to assume that you have your desire. You may feel you do not have the wisdom to find the means to get it, but you do. If it takes one thousand or ten thousand people to play their parts to bring you into the embodiment of what you have assumed you are, they will play their parts, knowingly or unknowingly. You don't have to be concerned as to who is going to aid you. Simply dare to assume you are what you want to be, and you will compel everyone to play their part to bring about your assumption. That is life.

77.

Now, in this world you can test it. You can test it, because he is the Power of God and the Wisdom of God. How do I test it? I dare to assume that I am what reason denies, and walk in the assumption that I AM that, and if I persist in that assumption, it will harden into fact. And if "by Him all things were made, and without Him was not anything made that was made, and then suddenly I am confronted with the thing itself, having assumed that it is, and I assumed it when reason denied the fact, haven't I found Him? If "by Him all things are made," and I dare to assume what my senses deny and reason denies it, and yet I persist in the assumption, and then eventually it hardens into fact . . well, did I not find the One Who makes things? And if "by Him all things are made, and without Him was not anything made that is made," and I have found exactly how I did it . . and I did it by simply assuming that I AM what I would like to be, even though at the moment of my assumption everything denies that I could possibly be that, and then I became that . . well then, I have found Jesus.

78.

While you are here you can test your creative power based upon your desires. You may desire something you think you cannot afford, or you don't have the time or the know-how to enjoy it. You can think of a thousand reasons why its possession is impossible; but . . hearing that imagination creates reality . . you can imagine you have it. But to imagine is not enough; you must have faith enough in your imaginal act to believe in its reality. When you imagine you are the person you want to be, you must firmly believe you already are it; then wait in faith for your assumption to appear in your world, for that imaginal act has its own appointed hour. It will ripen and flower. If it seems long to you . . wait, for it is sure and will not be late.

The link between your imaginal act and its fulfillment is your faith, which is nothing more than your subjective appropriation of your objective hope. Hoping your desire . . subjectively appropriated . . is true, faith is your link to its objectivity. Act as God, and simply let it be so. God said: "Let there be light, Let the sun appear. Let the moon appear." After his imaginal act, God let everything appear, sustaining it by faith, knowing that without faith it is impossible to bring it to pass. "Faith is the assurance of things hoped for, the evidence of things not yet seen." If you have faith in the reality of your imaginal act, it must objectify itself in your world.

79.

You can put God to the test, and if He proves himself in the testing then you will know God is your own wonderful human imagination. If you want the joy of marriage, a love affair, or a romance, you can test God by assuming the one you desire is with you now. And to the degree you persist in that assumption, it will be yours to experience. Do not be concerned as to how or when it will happen; simply persist in the assumption that it has happened, and when it does you will know who God is.

80.

Look in a mirror and you will see your face reflected there, but you have another mirror which you can look into. That is the mirror of your friends; if they heard your good news, their faces would reflect it would they not? Assume your desire is now a fact. Feel its substance and reality. Then let your friends see you in that state. They are your living mirror.

Now persevere in that state and do not turn away and quickly forget what you are like. Walk through this door tonight in the assumption that you are the man (or woman) you want to be. It doesn't make any difference if the outside denies it; you have seen the expression on the faces of your friends and heard their congratulations on the inside, with faith. Now, carry this feeling into the deep and persevere. Conjure a living mirror of friends and acquaintances who have heard your good news and accepted it as permanent. See your face reflected in theirs. If they love you, you will see empathy. They will be rejoicing because of your good fortune. Now, persevere in that awareness and do not forget what you have seen in your living mirror. If you do, you will be blessed in the doing, as you are told in the first chapter of the Book of Psalms: "Blessed is the man who delights in the law of the Lord; the perfect law of liberty, for in all that he does, he prospers."

81.

When you say: "I AM," that is the Lord. Go tell them I AM hath sent you. So when you walk in the feeling "I AM so and so," it is not seen as yet, but that is something you are bringing to the Lord, and the more you feel it to be real, the more natural it becomes. Then it clothes itself in external facts, but the external fact is not the truth of it. Truth and fact oppose each other. Truth does not depend upon fact. Truth depends upon the intensity of your imagination. Therefore, if I actually am intense about it, that is true. I might tomorrow find a corresponding fact to bear witness . . but, as I said earlier, let me not continue in that assumption and the fact will fade, proving it was not reality at all. Reality was in my assumption, and so truth depends not upon fact, but upon the intensity of imagination.

82.

God's law was established in the beginning, as everything must bear fruit after its own kind. If it's a pear tree, it bears pears; a plum tree bears plums, and an apple tree, apples. Bones represent the law of identical harvest. Assuming you are known or unknown, wanted or unwanted, wealthy or poor, your assumption is your seed and because of God's law you will bring forth that which you have assumed you are.

83.

For we are told: "All things were made by him, and without him was not made anything that was made." Then we discovered that we could imagine ourselves to be what we want to be and . . remaining faithful, remaining loyal to that assumption . . it became an external fact in our world. If "all things were made by him, and without him was not anything made that was made," and we did this as an experiment and it worked, well then . . we discovered God! And he wasn't some being in space who would return. We found him in ourselves as our wonderful human imagination.

84.

Tonight I give you a principle: God is the great artist, who .. as your own wonderful human imagination .. is perfecting his work through the ages in the making of his own image in you. Do you have an image? Name it. Now, are you willing to simply assume that you have it, and wait for its objectification?

Every image has its own appointed hour to ripen and flower. If it be long, wait, for its appearance is sure and will not be late. Are you willing to wait for the happiness you now seek, or are you going to try to go on the outside and make it so? If you are willing to apply this principle and let it happen, you will become the successful businessman, doctor, minister, or whatever you desire to be. If you will assume your desire and live there as though it were true, no power on earth can stop it from becoming a fact, because you are God and your only opponent is yourself.

85.

We must act on the assumption that we already possess that which we desire, for all that we desire is already present within us. It only waits to be claimed. That it must be claimed is a necessary condition by which we realize our desires. Our prayers are answered if we assume the feeling of the wish fulfilled and continue in that assumption.

86.

Let us assume that this is a dream and everything is perfect. You are happy and content and all is right in your world. Then persuade yourself of the reality of your assumption. Don't do anything to make it so; just trust the dreamer in you to bring it to pass, for the power who assumed your desire is the Lord Jesus Christ, and all things are possible to him. Your assumption, though false in the sense that it is denied by your senses and reason, if persisted in will harden into fact in such a normal, natural way that you will think it would have happened anyway. That is the dream.

When imagination fulfills itself so naturally, it is easy to question that your assumption had anything to do with it; but I tell you it could not have happened without your assumption, for your awareness is the one and only cause of the phenomena of your life.

87.

And so, you need money? No, you don't. I share with you what I have discovered. All you need is to assume the feeling of the wish fulfilled. That's all that you need to do, because He is within you. Though asleep, He still grants the wish, for that is His Law. Assume the feeling of the wish fulfilled. Though reason denies it, though your senses deny it, don't waiver in that assumption. You assume it. Persist in the assumption, and that assumption will harden into reality, if you call reality these concrete things in the world. But really, these are the shadows.

The reality was the invisible state that projected itself into what we can the "reality"; but the real Reality was invisible. Have faith. Have confidence in that invisible state. Assume it, "wear" it; it will externalize itself.

88.

If you define your aim as a noble, generous, secure, kindly individual . . knowing that all things are states of consciousness . . you can easily tell whether you are faithful to your aim in life by watching your reactions to the daily events of life. If you are faithful to your ideal, your reactions will conform to your aim, for you will be identified with your aim and, therefore, will be thinking from your aim. If your reactions are not in harmony with your ideal, it is a sure sign that you are separated from your ideal and are only thinking of it.

Assume that you are the loving one you want to be, and notice your reactions throughout the day in regard to that assumption; for your reactions will tell you the state from which you are operating.

89.

"There is a moment in every day," said Blake, "that Satan cannot find, nor can his watch fiends find it. But the industrious find this moment and it multiply and when it once is found, it renovates every moment of the day if rightly placed."

Now, by the word "Satan," he simply means doubt. Doubt cannot find it. I desire a certain state in this world. Reason tells me it's difficult; my friends tell me it's impossible; and so if I doubt that I could ever realize it, that's the voice of Satan speaking to me. He's always challenging God. God is my own wonderful human imagination. That's God. So the protagonists are God and Satan . . simply faith and doubt.

Can I imagine that I am the one that I would like to be and remain faithful to that assumption as though it were true. If I can and remember that assumption and when I did it, then I will see when it happens in my world the relationship between the natural effect and its spiritual cause. The spiritual cause was that moment of assumption.

90.

In the 11th chapter of Luke, it is said that Jesus was praying when one of his disciples said: "Lord, teach us to pray," at which time he gave them the Lord's Prayer. Now, the Lord's Prayer that you and I have is translated from the Latin, which does not have the imperative passive mood necessary to convey the meaning of the prayer. In its original Greek, the prayer is like brazen impudence, for the imperative passive mood is a standing order, something to be done absolutely and continuously. In other words, "Thy will be done," becomes "Thy will must be being done." And "Thy kingdom come" becomes "Thy kingdom must be being restored."

That is not what is being taught, however, as he taught in the form of a parable such as: "Which of you who has a friend would go to him at midnight and say to him, 'Friend, lend me three loaves, for a friend of mine has arrived on a journey and I have nothing to set before him,' and from within he says, 'Do not bother me; the door is shut and my children are in bed. I cannot rise and give you anything.' Yet I tell you, although he will not rise because he is a friend, yet because of his importunity, he will rise and give him whatever he needs." The word importunity means brazen impudence. In other words, he would not take No for an answer!

Jesus was not teaching a disciple on the outside how to pray. He was telling you how to adjust your thinking so you will not take No for an answer. In the story the friend knew what he wanted. He assumed he had it and continued to assume he had it until his assumption took on the feeling of reality and he got it. This is how you find God in yourself, by being persistent in your assumption.

91.

The ideal you serve and hope to achieve is ready and waiting for a new incarnation, but it is incapable of birth unless you offer it human parentage. You must assume that you already are what you hope to be and live as though you were.

You must know, like Dr. Millikan did, that your assumption, though false to the outer world, will harden into fact by your persistence. The perfect man judges not after appearances, but judges righteously. He hears what he wants to hear and sees only the good. Knowing the truth that sets him free, he is lead to all good.

92.

But I do know that God's law reflects all the way down to this world of Caesar. I do not know how long it takes for each egg to hatch in a nest, but I do know each one will hatch in its own time. And so it is with an assumption. If I desire to be wealthy, I may not know how long it will take me to reach the conviction that I possess great wealth, but when I feel wealth is mine I have conceived. Conception is my end.

The length of time between my desire and its conception depends entirely upon my inner conviction that it is done. A horse takes twelve months, a cow nine months, a chicken twenty-one days, so there are intervals of time; but it comes down to the simple fact that the truth concerning every concept is known by the feeling of its certainty. When you know it, not a thing can disturb your knowingness!

93.

If you would like to live in a lovely apartment, claim you do. You may think you can't afford the one you want, but that thought is an imaginal act. I would suggest, instead of thinking you can't afford it, to simply sleep in that apartment tonight mentally, accepting the fact that you have all the funds necessary to pay for it.

Persist and the world will respond. You will get the money needed to live there. The world does not cause, it only responds to your imaginal acts, for only God acts and God is in you as your own wonderful human imagination. Now, before you judge it, try it. If you do, you cannot fail, and when you prove imagination in the testing, share the good news with your brothers. Tell everyone you meet how the world works. You do not have to have a proper educational or social background to apply this principle; and you cannot fail, for an assumption, though false, if persisted in will harden into fact.

94.

"The story of Jesus is a persistent assumption that you are what you want to be, that things are as you desire them to be." This is true, for unless you believe that you are the being you now worship on the outside, you remain desiring and die in your sins of unfulfilled desires. You've got to begin to believe that you are Jesus Christ, the Word of God, which . . having gone out will not return empty, but will fulfill your purpose and accomplish that which you sent yourself to do. What is that? To fulfill scripture. That's all you are here for.

95.

Believe every precept literally, for it will be fulfilled literally. Believe that all things are possible to you and that you are what you want to be. Persist in that assumption and it will harden into fact. Having assumed the life you now live, no one can take it from you but yourself! You have the power to lay it down by no longer being conscious of it, and the power to pick it up again through consciousness.

96.

Ask for wealth in the name of God by saying: "I AM wealthy." You cannot point outside of self and call upon God's name. If I am in an impoverished state and desire the state of wealth, I must dare to assume I AM wealthy. The Torah is a discussion between Jehovah and Pharaoh, or faith and doubt. You must have the faith of assumption that you are the man you want to be in order to become it. Your desires will never come to pass if you believe the denials displayed by your reason and outer senses. As you walk in the assumption that your desire is fulfilled, you are calling upon the name of God and conjuring that which you are assuming. You must dare to assume wealth, if that is your objective.

97.

If you desire health, you must assume it, even though the doctor's reasoning world produces proof to the contrary. You must be ever aware that they are not your God, that there is only one God and his name is I AM! When you point to another as an authority in your world, you are transferring the power that belongs to God to an idol. Now, if you call for anything with the name of God, and his name is I AM, and you say I AM . . are you not your own maker?

God is, for I AM! I kill and I make alive, I wound and I heal. I create the light and I form the darkness and besides me there is no other God. Whatever I want, I must assume the full responsibility for it. If I want to conjure health and the doctors tell me I cannot overcome my illness and I believe them, I have made my choice and must accept the responsibility for it. But if I dare to assume health, God is proclaiming it, for he has no name other than I AM!

This is the grand revelation found in the third chapter, the 14th verse, of Exodus. "Go and tell them `I AM has sent me to you.' "Whatever you declare, is; for God's name is any form of the verb to be, whether it is I AM, I was, or I will be.

98.

The story of Jesus is a complete and undeviating persistence in the assumption that you are what you want to be. If you haven't experienced wealth and that is what you want, persistently assume . . I AM wealthy." If you have not experienced fame, assume you are famous, but . . The day will come," saith the Lord . . when I will send a famine upon you. It will not be a hunger for bread or a thirst for water, but for the hearing of my Word." If that hunger hasn't come to you, then take the same story of Jesus and fulfill your every desire.

99.

"All that you behold, though it appears without it is within, of which this world of mortality is but a shadow." If you will but enter a state in your imagination, and assume its truth, the outer world will respond to your assumption, for it is your shadow, forever bearing witness to your inner imaginal activity.

100.

I tell you it is possible to be anything you want to be, for the believer and the God of the universe are one. Don't divorce yourself from God, for he is your I AMness. Believe in your I AMness, for if you do not you will never fulfill your desire. Only by assuming you already are the one you would like to be will you achieve it. It's just as simple as that.

101.

If you dare to assume you are what you want to be, your inner conviction, your feeling of certainty will bring it to pass. When you embrace the desired state, you have assumed its impregnation, and its fulfillment has its own appointed hour. It will ripen and flower. If the state is slow in objectifying itself wait, for it is sure and will not be late.

102.

Don't feel that you are better than someone else, you are creative power. Stand upon your tower and watch to see what God will say and how you will answer. Do this by assuming you are the person you want to be and seeing what you would see if your assumption was real. Remain there until you feel its certainty, until you reach the point of satisfaction, until you are convinced of its truth; and although the world may collapse around you, you will become that which you have assumed you are.

103.

So, when I say "Awake, O Sleeper," I'm simply appealing to everyone here to awake to God's Law. For it is a law established in the beginning . . the Law of the Identical Harvest. You can't plant one thing and reap another. You could now sit here tonight in the assumption that you are . . well, exactly as you want to be. I would not define for what you ought to want; I will ask you: What do you want?

When you know exactly what you would like to be, and you deliberately assume that you are it, you've planted that seed. And in due season you are going to reap that harvest. Therefore, if you're going to reap it, reap it wisely by planting wisely.

104.

Now, if you keep this law, you don't have to broadcast what you want; you simply assume that you have it, for . . although your reasonable mind and outer senses deny it . . if you persist in your assumption your desire will become your reality. There is no limit to your power of belief, and all things are possible to him who believes. Just imagine what an enormous power that is. You don't have to be nice, good, or wise, for anything is possible to you when you believe that what you are imagining is true. That is the way to success.

105.

If you want to test God, you may. Your immortal eyes and ears need not be open to test your creative power. Simply assume you are the one you want to be. Remain faithful to your assumption and, although everything denies it, you will become it. It does not matter who you are or what the world thinks of you; anything is possible to the "I" of imagination.

106.

Remember, creative power will not operate itself. Knowing what to do is not enough. You, imagination's operant power, must be willing to assume that things are as you desire them to be before they can ever come to pass.

107.

Take the idea that you want to embody, and assume that you are already it. Lose yourself in feeling this assumption is solidly real. As you give it this sense of reality, you have given it the blessing which belongs to the objective world, and you do not have to aid its birth any more than you have to aid the birth of a child or a seed you plant in the ground. The seed you plant grows unaided by a man, for it contains within itself all the power and all the plans necessary for self-expression.

108.

Creation is finished and you have free will to choose the state you will occupy. Therefore, it is important to determine the ideas from which you think. Any concept that is accepted as true will externalize itself in your outer world. Choice of what you will focus your attention upon is the only free will that you can exercise. Once a thought is accepted and charged with feeling, the creative power within proceeds to externalize it.

Whether your assumptions are conscious or unconscious, they direct all action to their fulfillment. It is a delusion that, other than assuming the feeling of the wish fulfilled, you can do anything to aid its realization. Your own wonderful human imagination determines the means it will use to bring your assumptions to fruition.

109.

"Whatever you desire, believe you have received it and you will." Knowing what you want, assume you have it and let no one divert you. Do your father's will, believing in the feeling of your wish fulfilled. Try it, for this simple principle will not fail you. But remember: you are its power, as it does not operate itself. I can tell you how to move into another state, but you must move into it. No one can do it for you. You see, states are permanent and it is up to you to get out of the state you are now in if it is undesirable to you.

110.

Night after night, sleep as though you are the man . . the woman . . that you would be or that you would like to be. And then, if tomorrow does not bring it to pass, it doesn't matter. There are intervals of time between the assumption and its fulfillment. It's like generation. So, if you dare to assume it, give it time. And then some bridge of incidents will be built for you without your conscious knowledge of it, and it will lead you across that bridge to the fulfillment of your assumption in a way that you do not know.

111.

I ask you to take me seriously. Imagination will fulfill itself, so do not limit yourself by anything that is now happening, no matter what it is. Knowing what you want, conceive a scene which would imply you have it. Persuade yourself of its truth and walk blindly on in that assumption. Believe it is real. Believe it is true and it will come to pass. Imagination will not fail you if you dare to assume and persist in your assumption, for imagination will fulfill itself in what your life becomes.

112.

This I do know. By simply assuming I am the man I would like to be and mentally acting in harmony with my assumption, I have aided the birth of my desires and brought them to pass. I have played the game of assumption time and time again and it has never failed me. When someone asks something of me I simply assume they have what they want, then whatever needs to take place in this world will take place and bring it to pass, but where did the desires' fulfillment originate but in my imagination?

113.

When you know what you want, assume you have it. Believe your assumption is true. Look at your world mentally and see your fulfilled desire. Do this and you are calling forth a response to your thoughts, and in the not distant future you will find yourself physically occupying the state imagined.

114.

Try to remember that there is no limit to God's creative power, or your power of belief. Persuade yourself that things are as you desire them to be. Fall asleep in that assumption, as that is your act of faith. Tomorrow the world will begin to change, to make room for the garment of your assumption. If it takes one person or ten thousand to aid the birth of your assumption, they will come. You will not need their consent or permission, because the world is dead and what would be the purpose in asking dead people to help you? Simply know what you want, animate the scene and those playing their parts will begin to move towards the fulfillment of your desire.

115.

Now, what are you assuming that you are? You can assume anything in this world, for the Being-assuming is God. Can you believe in the reality of your assumption? Can you believe that which at the moment your reason denies and your senses deny? Can you believe it? If you can believe it, no power in the world can stop it from objectifying in this world of ours . . but no one.

116.

Without the help of any man or government you could lose everything you possess and become dependent upon society. All you need do is enter the state of poverty. Or again: without asking for help you could assume wealth by occupying the state. Remain faithful to it and you will discover that the state has its own way of externalizing itself. You must, however, give the desired state occupancy.

117.

Always lift the mind to that which we seek. This is easily done by assuming the feeling of the wish fulfilled. How would you feel if your prayer were answered? Well, assume that feeling until you experience in imagination what you would experience in reality, if your prayer were answered. Prayer means getting into action mentally. It means holding the attention upon the idea of the wish fulfilled until it fills the mind and crowds all other ideas out of the consciousness.

118.

In the meanwhile, take what you know of this law, and use it towards your own personal good fortune in the world of Caesar. It's simple. Go to the end and assume the feeling of the wish fulfilled. Don't ask anyone to help you. Ask no one if it is right. If you like it, assume you have it. Remain faithful to your assumption, and that Being who is going to erupt in you will take you to that end. If you find yourself moving from your fulfilled desire, go back to it, and once more assume the feeling of the wish fulfilled. Do this and your assumption will harden into fact.

119.

Appearances confirm our former habitual patterns of thought. That which you imagine yourself to be today will project itself in your world tomorrow. Persistence in assuming that you are the person you wish to be, despite your present circumstances, is the only condition imposed upon you to embody that ideal.

120.

So this lesson was given us in the beginning. Whatever you are beholding in your mind's eye, you will produce in your outer world. It is just as simple as that. I hope you are beholding your fulfilled desire in your mind's eye; for scripture tells you that: "Whatever you desire, believe you have received it and you will." This is telling you that, to the degree you are self-persuaded, you will become what you have assumed you are.

121.

As you dwell upon this power vested in you, you will discover it will help you far beyond your wildest dreams. You will realize that you do not need the help of anyone. All you need do is assume you have what you want. Then dare to walk in that assumption; and if it takes a thousand people to aid its birth, they will appear and play their parts, not knowing why or what they do.

122.

Take the challenge of scripture and assume the feeling of the wish fulfilled . . not only for yourself, but for your family and friends. When you imagine for another, you are really giving it to yourself, as there is no other. The whole vast world is only yourself pushed out.

4 Lectures on The Law of Assumption

Persistent Assumption . . 03-18-1968
Persistent Assumption. . 06-18-1968
You Dare To Assume . . 06-19-1970
Radio Talk - The Law of Assumption . . July 1951

Lecture 1 of 4

Persistent Assumption .. 03-18-1968

I tell you a truth: There is nothing greater than your own wonderful human imagination! It is He who inspired Blake, Shakespeare, and Einstein, for there is only one spirit in the universe! "Hear, O Israel, the Lord our God, the Lord is One." That one spirit is the human imagination! When Blake was asked what he thought of the divinity of Christ he answered: "Christ is the only God, but so AM I and so are you." Don't think of Christ as someone greater than yourself. He is the only God, but so AM I and so are you! Don't consider yourself less than Christ, for there is only God, who is your own wonderful human imagination.

Daring to assume that all things are possible to imagine, put this one reality to the extreme test by assuming you are the person you would like to be. Your reasonable mind and outer senses may deny it; but I promise you: if you will persist, you will receive your assumption. Believe me, you are the same God who created and sustains the universe, but are keyed low; so you must be persistent if you would bring about a change.

In the Book of Luke, the story is told of a man who came to a house at the midnight hour, and said: "A friend has arrived who is hungry. Would you let me have three loaves of bread?" The man upstairs replied: "It is midnight. My children are in bed asleep and I cannot come down and give you what you want." Then this statement is made: "But because of the man's importunity, he was given all that he desired." The word "importunity" means "brazen impudence." Having a desire, the man would not take no for an answer!

When you know what you want, you don't ask God as though he were another; you ask your individual self to bring about your desire, for you are He! And God . . your own wonderful human imagination . . will respond when you will not take no for an answer, as your denial is spoken from within and there is no other. It is within your own being that you persist in assuming you have received what you want. The story is, even though it was midnight and the family was asleep, the father came down and gave what was needed.

The God of a Blake, a Shakespeare, or an Einstein, does not differ from the God housed in you, as there is only one human imagination. There cannot be two. He is not a dual God. You and your imagination are not less than anyone, but you must learn to be persistent.

A friend recently shared a vision with me, in which I appeared and said: "The story of Jesus is persistent assumption." If this is true, and we are told to imitate him as a dear child, I must dare to assume I am the being I want to be. I must continue in that assumption until that which I have assumed is objectively realized. And if I am one with everyone, how can anyone be greater than I? Do not believe that someone is greater than you because of some influx of spirit or validity. Your imagination is the only God, and there is no other being greater than He! Claim you are what you want to be. Persist in that assumption. Continue to assume that role until that which you have assumed is reflected in your world.

Although the churches teach that another, greater than yourself, said: "Unless you believe that I AM He, you will die in your sins" . . these words were spoken by the human imagination! And because imagination is one, and you can't get away from that oneness, don't think of another. Accept these words in the first person, present tense; for unless you believe that you already are what you want to be, you will die in your sins by leaving your desire unfulfilled. If you do not believe you are all imagination, you will continue in your former belief, worshipping a God on the outside and not within.

On this level, we are fragmented, but we are all that one imagination. The word "Elohim" is a compound unity of one made up of others. Although we seem to be many, in the most intimate manner possible, we are one! On this level, you and I are keyed low for purposes beyond our wildest dreams, yet called upon to make the effort to rise above it. This is done in a physical, scientific, and artistic sense, as we begin to discover and express our human imagination. We rise above this level through the act of assumption; for an assumption, though false, if persisted in will harden into fact. As William Blake said: "If the fool will persist in his folly he will become wise."

There is nothing God cannot do! Do not think that one who is fabulously rich has an influx of spirit which differs from yours. He is imagining wealth, either wittingly or unwittingly; but you can do it knowingly. If he does not know what he is doing, he can lose his wealth and not know how to recover it. I am asking you, regardless of your financial situation, to assume wealth, knowingly. If, tomorrow you would again return to your former state, bring wealth back by claiming "I AM wealthy," for there is only one God. He who creates poverty also creates wealth, as there is no other creator.

The world thinks of numberless gods, but there is only one. That one is your own wonderful human imagination. Possessing only one son, when imagination awakens, God's only begotten son will reveal you as God. The same thing will happen to another, then another . . and eventually everyone will see the same son, who will reveal the individual as God the Father.

This world is a play, where divine imagination becomes human imagination by inserting himself into an olive skin, a black skin, a white skin, and a red skin. Although we appear to be different, we all will see God's only begotten son . . proving that there is only one God. The purpose behind the play is to expand imagination's creative power. Here we are fragmented into numberless parts, destined to gather ourselves together into the one God, the one Father of all.

Begin now to actively, constantly, use your imagination; for as you prove its creative power on this level, you are awakening to a higher level and birth into the spirit world where you know yourself to be God. Prove to yourself that you are God by feeling your desire is now an accomplished fact. Listen to your friends talk about you. Are they rejoicing because of your good fortune, or are they expressing envy? Imagine their words are true. Persist in imagining they are true. Continue to imagine your desire is already an accomplished fact; and when it is objectively realized, proof will be yours.

Think of something lovely you would like to give another. Then ask yourself if you gave it to him and he wouldn't accept it, would you want to keep it for yourself? If, for instance, you gave a friend a million dollars and he would not accept it, would you be willing to keep it? I'm sure you would. Then imagine giving the money to him, then give to others in the same way. You may not even have a bank account; but you can still give, because there is no one to give to but yourself! There is only God whose name is I AM!

"Hear, O Israel, the Lord our God, the Lord is one." This great confession of faith is recorded in the sixth chapter, the fourth verse of the Book of Deuteronomy. The Lord is not two, not a dozen . . just one. If I say "I AM" that's one, but if I say "we are" I am speaking of many.

Jesus' name is "I AM." He is not some superior being other than yourself. He is the inspiration for everything you write, be it trivia or profound. Inspiration does not come from some other being, because there cannot be another. When you sit down to write, the thoughts come from your own being! It is nonsense to think of some other being as possessing you.

The great poets . . the Shakespeare's, the Blake's . . had no great spiritual influx moving in them that is greater than the spiritual influx in you. It cannot be, for there is no one greater than self! When someone tells me he is under the influence of some greater power, I tell him that is not possible. The inspiration is coming from the depths of his own soul. Perhaps you have an item you would like to advertise. As you think of what your customer needs, the answer will come from the depth of your own soul, and you will know what needs to be said to promote your product. You do not receive some influx of spirit outside of yourself, for there is no one greater! There is only God, and God is one!

In the Book of Psalms, you are told to; "Commune with your own self." Sit quietly. Be at peace with yourself and suddenly thoughts will begin to flow within you, from God. In the beginning you were God! And in the end, you and I and the whole vast world of billions will be re-gathered into the one God. One imagination fell into this fragmented world of seeming others, yet the whole is within each one of us. A man's enemies are those of his own household, for they are all within him. Not knowing this, man fights within himself until he realizes there is no other, just himself. Then he tells others in the hope he can convince himself. And as he rises from within, he is called back into the one being he was before that the world was. The fall into division was deliberate for God's expansion into unity.

There was no other way to expand your creative power but by falling into limitation and overcoming it. As you fell, your being fragmented. I saw this so clearly in vision. First, a rock appeared. Then it fragmented and as it gathered together it took the shape of a man sitting in the lotus posture, meditating, glowing. And I knew I was looking at myself! And as it began to glow like the sun, I awoke in my apartment in New York City.

I am telling you what I have done, what I have seen, and what I have experienced. Each one of us has a being within who is meditating us. The being in you and the being in all, form the one perfect being, who fell and fragmented himself. One day, everyone's living being will unite into the one God, who fell and fragmented himself. Do you know what you would you like to be? Dare to assume it and, for one week, claim: "I have assumed I am the one I want to be. I am still assuming I am, and I will continue to assume I am until that which I have assumed is objectively realized." Fall asleep assuming it is true, and let that living being in you give it life.

God the Father is dreaming in the depth of your soul. It is he who began a good work in you, and it is he who will bring it to completion at the day of Jesus Christ. On that day you will be brought to the same perfection as the Father in you, for God is dreaming himself into a greater image of himself and you, the dreamer, are dreaming yourself into the image of yourself.

While you are here, you can assume any desire for yourself and those you love. Then you can dare to believe in what you have assumed. And if you continue your assumption, you will express it. But you must believe, or you will die in your sins. Always talking to yourself, you are telling yourself that unless you believe you are the man you want to be, you will remain being the man you don't want to be, thereby dying in your sins.

To believe in another . . whether he appear as a Blake, a Shakespeare or an Einstein . . you have a false God. You must believe in yourself or die in your sins! You must believe that God actually became you that you may become God . . for he did. His name is I AM and unless you say within yourself: "I AM what I want to be" and believe it, you will remain saying within yourself: "I wish I were what I want to be" and die in your frustration (your sin). I urge to you learn how to believe in yourself. It may appear to be difficult at first, but not when you are willing to go out on a limb and try it.

I admire the great, inspired poets. Shakespeare is marvelous. Blake is altogether wonderful, and Einstein truly great in his field. These were inspired men; but they did not have any influx of spirit that made them greater than your human imagination, for their imagination and your imagination are one grand, divine imagination, imagining! Their work did not come from something outside of themselves, but from their own imagination, awakening. That same imagination is yours because there is only one spirit. The spirit of man is one with the spirit of the universe and there is no other!

Start now to capture the feeling of being this one spirit. Fall asleep in the feeling that you are God, and as you come hurtling back from the depth of unconsciousness toward this level, you will have numberless crazy little dreams based upon this person you are coming through. You will give importance to these dreams; but oh, what depths you will reach in that which is unconscious relative to this level!

Let no one frighten you, for you are an immortal being who cannot die. Although I have awakened to my Godhood before you, I am no better because I got there first, for there is no such thing as being first. Everyone is moving toward that level, and no one can fail. And when all have returned, what joy will be expressed as we form the one body, the one spirit, the one Lord, the one God and Father of all! Everyone will have the vision and prove to himself that he is God the Father.

I urge you to apply this principle and cushion yourself against the normal blows of life. If your friends and loved ones cannot believe, cushion them anyway; for no matter what you leave them here, you are not going to stop the blows given by the depth of their own being. If you left each friend one hundred thousand dollars, you would cushion them for the moment; but the depth of their being will continue to take them through experiences, in order to awaken to the knowledge that they are the father of God's only begotten son, David.

The world is searching for the cause of the phenomena of life, not knowing he is their very self. What responsibility is yours when you discover that your awareness is the cause of everything that has happened, is happening, and will happen to you. But when you realize that you are causing all the blows, the heartaches, and pains, that happen to you, you will begin to change your thinking; and as you do, scripture will unfold in you.

Now let us go into the Silence.

Lecture 2 of 4

Persistent Assumption .. 06-18-1968

Now, you and I look out on a world, and we think of the great men and women who are publicized in the world, and many of them are altogether wonderful. We speak of the great poets, the scientists, the businessmen . . all these fellows in the world, and we think, "Well now, there must be something different about them."

Now, may I tell you? There's not a thing different about them. I want to convince you this night, if I can, that this inspiration that we think the poet has, the scientist, the great businessman, is not an influx of a spirit that is different. It's not different from the individual's own wonderful human imagination, because there's nothing greater. So, there is no greater influx of Spirit into a Blake, into a Shakespeare, into an Einstein, into you, than your own wonderful human imagination, for there is nothing greater. There is only one Spirit in man and the Universe!

"Hear, O Israel, the Lord our God, the Lord is one"

There is not a greater spirit than your own wonderful human imagination.

In a little conversation that Blake had with his friend, Crabb Robinson, Robinson asked him what he thought of the divinity of Christ and he answered, "Christ is the only God, but so am I, and so are you. Now don't forget it! When you think of Christ, you are making something bigger than yourself . . something greater than yourself. Blake said, "Christ is the only God, but so am I." If Christ is the only

God "and so am I," I make myself one with him. Then he turns to Crabb Robinson and says, "So are you." So don't forget it.

If you forget this, you make yourself less than the One. You can't be less than the One; there is only One. There is only God in this world! There is nothing but God, and God is your own wonderful human imagination. That is God.

Now tonight, let us put it to the extreme test. If God is the only Reality . . you can't have two, not two gods . . and He is my own wonderful human imagination, and "All things are possible to God." All right, how would I go about proving it? For I am called upon to test it!

"Test it." I will dare to assume that I am the man that I would like to be. At the moment, reason denies it, my senses deny it; but I will dare to assume that I am it. Now, what am I told in Scripture that I should do? Well, listen to it carefully. These are stories told in Scripture of the necessity of persistence because we are "keyed low." The same God . . the God that created the Universe and sustains it by His Creative Power . . is the God that is sitting here in these chairs tonight. But here for a divine purpose, the same God is "keyed low."

So, would I bring about a change in my world? Then I am called upon in Scripture to be persistent, because I see this world, and everything that I have assumed is denied . . as I assume it . . by the things round about me. Now listen to these stories as told in Scripture.

A man came at the midnight hour to his friend, and he said, "A friend has called, 'I have no bread. Would you just let me have three loaves of bread?' and the one who opened the upstairs window said to him, 'It is midnight, and my children are asleep in bed. I cannot come down and give you what you want.'"

And the story as told us in the book of Luke is this: he would not come down; but because of this man's importunity, he came down and gave him all that he needed. Well, the word translated importunity means brazen impudence. He would not take "No" for an answer.

I don't ask you, as an individual . . I don't ask any outside god; as an individual, I am asking my Self to bring this thing to pass. That is what I am actually saying, because I am speaking to the only God. There is only God! And if God is my own wonderful human imagination, to whom am I going to turn when It doesn't respond . . when I don't take "No" for an answer?

So, within my own being, I am assuming that I have received exactly what I need. Now the story is that even though it was midnight, he was in bed with his children, still he came down and gave him what he needed. You do not take "No" for an answer, because there is no "other," may I tell you? I don't care whether you speak of a Shakespeare whom you think, "My god, isn't he marvelous!" . . and he is; and the Blakes of the world, and they are marvelous; and the Einsteins, and they are marvelous. But the God of an Einstein does not differ from the God of your own wonderful human imagination. There is only God! There can't be two.

"Hear, O Israel, the Lord our God, the Lord is One." He is not a dual God . . one God. So, your own wonderful human imagination is this God, and you are not less than any being in this world. But you have to be persistent.

When Benny came home last night, he said, "Neville, have you forgotten my vision? When I was talking to someone and you came into the picture, and this one said to you . . and he asked this very simple question! 'Tell us the story of Jesus,' and you automatically said, 'The story of Jesus is persistent assumption.'"

Persistent assumption . . that's the story, for "Jesus" means "salvation." Well, if persistent assumption is the story of Jesus, I must dare to assume that I AM what I want to be. I must continue in the assumption that I AM it until that which I have assumed is objectively realized. That is the story of Jesus. For if I am one with anything in this world, and he is great and she is great, and I am not, and yet we are one, well, now . . what is this fragmented being when there is only one? I tell you, that One is your own wonderful human imagination, and don't let anyone in this world tell you that an Einstein or a Shakespeare is greater because of some influx of a spirit of greater validity than their own wonderful human imagination, because there is no greater. Your imagination is God, and there is no other God. And there can be no other greater Being than your own wonderful human imagination.

Now you begin to imagine it. Well, now I will say, "I have assumed that I am the man that I want to be." I am still assuming that I AM He, and I will continue to assume that I AM He until that which I have assumed is objectively realized, as told us in the 8th chapter of John:

"Unless you believe I AM He" . . now when you read it, you think as you are taught by the churches of the world, that another greater than yourself is speaking, it is not another greater than you speaking, telling you unless you believe He is . . it's your Self speaking. There is only God, because God is One and you can't get away from the Oneness: don't think of "another."

So, these words must be accepted in the first person, present tense, so "unless you believe that I AM He, you will die in your sins" . . you'll miss the mark. I must believe that I am the man that I want to be. If I do not believe that I am that very being so that I can say, "Well, I AM He," then I will continue what I formerly believed myself to be. This is the story of Scripture. So, we are all one . . everyone here. You and I are one, because there can't be two. On this level, for a purpose, we are fragmented; but I am sent to tell you that we are not really many. We are one.

The word "Elohim" is a compound unity: one made up of others. So here it seems to be "others," but you and I are not really two, three, four, or many. We are one, in the most intimate manner that you've ever known, without loss of identity!

So, I ask you this night to simply dwell upon it, and simply try it. Just try it. It will never in Eternity fail you.

Here is a letter that came to me this past week. She said in her letter, "I was awakened by the laughter of my husband. He was laughing . . the sweetest laughter I have ever heard . . just a laugh. I have never heard him laugh like this. So I awoke, and here he's laughing a peculiar but wonderful laughter. And I said to myself, 'Well, he's undoubtedly dreaming something that is altogether wonderful.'

"And then the next morning he said to me, 'I had the loveliest dream last night. I dreamt that you were telling me it's so easy to believe that I AM God.'"

Now I am going to tell him, . . he is here tonight alone; she isn't here . . tell her, and you too, read it: the 126th

Psalm. There is your answer, only six verses. That was the laughter of God.

She said, "I heard a voice coming from within me saying, 'You've just heard the laughter of God!'"

Well, read the 126th Psalm, when all returned to Zion . . those who were left. They all left, and then they all are brought back into Zion, and here, you hear the laughter of God.

> When the LORD restored the fortunes of Zion,
> We were like those who dream.
>
> 2 Then our mouth was filled with laughter,
> And our tongue with shouts of joy;
> Then they said among the nations,
> "The LORD has done great things for them."
>
> 3 The LORD had done great things for us; we are glad.
>
> 4 Restore our fortunes, O LORD,
> Like the watercourses in the Negeb!
>
> 5 May those who sow in tears
> Reap with shouts of joy!
>
> 6 He that goes forth weeping,
> Bearing the seed for sowing,
> Shall come home with shouts of joy,
> Bringing his sheaves with him.

So, she heard him laugh in a way that she had never heard him before, and she had never heard this kind of a laughter. And she said to herself, "He's undoubtedly having a wonderful dream."

Then the next day he said to her, "I had a dream last night, and in my dream you were telling me that it is so easy to believe that I AM God!"

So, I tell you, you try it; this thing doesn't fail. There is only God. You are not something less than God; there is only God. And you and I, on this level, for purposes beyond the wildest dream . . we are keyed low; but we are called upon to make the effort to rise from this level. And so, we do it in a business sense, in a scientific sense, in an artistic sense; and so we begin to express this talent, which is our own wonderful human imagination, which is God. There is nothing but God!

So, I am called upon to assume that I am what I want to be, for, "An assumption, though false, if persisted in will harden into fact" [Sir Anthony Eden].

And as Blake said, "If the fool would persist in his folly, he would become wise" [from "The Marriage of Heaven and Hell"].

There is nothing that is impossible to God. So, don't say that something cannot be, . . I don't care what it is. You may see someone in the world, and he is a fabulously wealthy person. Well, so what! Do you think for one second some influx of Spirit that differs from the Being that you are, possessed him to make it? No. He either did it wittingly or unwittingly; may I tell you? But you can do it knowingly. If he does it unknowingly, which is the self, and he loses it tonight, he may not know how to recover it. I am asking you . . without having anything . . to do it knowingly.

So, should you tomorrow fall into another state, and you remember the story, you simply come back and simply bring it back into your world as you want it, and simply multiply it, and live graciously, for there's only one God, You can't conceive of . . well, you can conceive of a second god, but it is a stupid concept because there is no other god. When the world thinks of numberless gods, they are stupid. There's only one God, and that God is your own wonderful human imagination!

And the day will come that you will prove it. You will actually witness the One God! He sets Himself up at the very beginning, and this God has only one Son. And when you awaken and that Son calls you "Father" . . and therefore you are the father of the only Son of God . . well then, you know you are the only God! And then another one comes and another one comes; and eventually all come, and they see the same Son, and the same Son calls them "Father." Therefore, everyone is the same God the Father! And there aren't two of us.

There aren't two. Forget all the pigments of skin. All this is part of the "play." To put me into an olive skin and one in a black, black skin, and one in a white, white skin, and one in a red skin, it makes it appear as though we differ. And therefore, because we differ there must be different gods. And yet, all will have that same Son, and that one Son will call all of us . . regardless of sex . . "Father," proving that we are only one God. And the purpose behind it all is simply to create an expansion of His creative power.

So here we are scattered . . fragmented into numberless parts. And then all are gathered together into one God, one Father. I am going to ask you all to try it . . really try it, because if you really prove it on this level, may I tell you, you will never forget it! And you will be sustained by this level, and then, all of a sudden, you will be "born from above." I cannot tell you when, that is a secret hidden from us here.

If you tell me when you were "born from above," then I can tell you all the other events that will follow and when it will happen. I can tell you that because I have recorded it. But the actual "birth from above" remains a secret. "It comes like a thief in the night," but when it comes, you are "born from above," and you are God! You actually are God!

Now to prove that you are, you can create . . create in this simple, simple way: What would it be like if it were true? Just what would it be like? How would I feel if . . and then you name it. How would I feel if she, or he, were as I would like them to be? So, you would like something lovely to happen to them, and then you feel it.

Now, can you persist in that assumption? I imagine it to be so. I am still imagining it to be so, and I will continue to imagine that these things are as I have imagined them to be until it is objectively realized. Can I do that? Well, if I can, they will conform to it. Must I get their permission? I don't need their permission if we are one. That is what I want for them. I don't need their consent if it is something I would like for myself.

Always ask yourself, "Would I like it for myself?" If they reject it . . and they can reject it; but I mean, take it on this level. If they should reject it, would I willingly accept it? If I gave you a million dollars and you wouldn't take it, would I be willing to receive it again? I would. Well then, give it in that same way. And may I tell you? You can do it.

If you don't have one nickel in the bank . . if you don't have a bank account, you can do it, because there is no one but your Self. There is only God in this world. God is I AM. There is nothing but God!

"Hear, O Israel, the Lord our God, the Lord is One" . . the greatest prayer . . the greatest confession of faith that man could ever make. Read it in the 6th chapter of the book of Deuteronomy. I think it is the 4th verse. But oh! What a confession of faith!

"Hear, O Israel, the Lord our God, the Lord is One.

Not two, not a dozen . . just one.

Well, if He is One, what is One in this world? When I say, "I AM," that's one. If I say, "We are," that is multiple. But I AM, and that is His name. Don't forget it! Therefore, if I AM, even though, now, something is happening, I am not receiving from some superior being . . there is no superior being than my Self. The inspiration for anything I write . . if I sit down and write something that is all trivia or something that is altogether marvelous, it does not come from some other being who inspires me, because there is no greater Being. There cannot be another Being. So, when I sit down to write and I am in the mood, from my own Being it is coming out, and I am writing; but to say that some other Being is possessing me and they are taking over . . nonsense! No other Being: there can be no other Being.

So, the poet, the Shakespeares, the Blakes, the great writers of the world, or any writer in the world . . he doesn't have any Being influencing him, moving in some peculiar spiritual influx that is greater than himself. It cannot be. There is no one greater than himself. So, when someone tells me, "I was under the influence of something other than myself, it came from the outside" . . forget it. There isn't anyone; it's all coming from the depth of your own Soul.

So, all of a sudden, you are an advertiser, and you are sitting and wondering, "Now what does my customer need?"

And all of a sudden, from the depths of your own Soul it comes . . what you are going to say to promote that product. It isn't some influx of a spirit other than your Self. It can't be, because there is nothing greater than your Self. There is no other god; there is only one God.

So, you sit, and you are communing with Self, as told you in the Psalms: "Commune with your own Self." (Psalm 4:4) Well, you can sit on a chair or on your bed and commune with your own Self and be at peace. And all of a sudden the thing begins to flow from within, because there is only one God. And everything unfolds from within you: there is nothing but God. And in the end, you and I and the whole vast world of billions will be re-gathered into one body . . and, oh, what a joy!

One fell purposely into this fragmented world, seeing "others". . and fighting seeming "others" and the horror within one's Self that a man's enemies are "of his own household," meaning himself. He is fighting with himself, not knowing that everything in this world is himself. All of a sudden he realizes, there is no other . . just himself! And then he knows it, and he tells everyone in this world, in the hope that he can convince himself, because it is himself he's talking to, for there's only one God . . only one Being.

And then as he rises within himself, he once more coalesces into the One Being, knowing in the depth of his Being that everyone is going to coalesce into the same Being, and oh what a joy when all are raised into the One Being that was that Being before the Fall, And the Fall was a deliberate fall for the expansion of its power.

I can only expand my creative power by falling into this limitation and overcoming it. There is no other way to do it. And as I fell, I fragmented my being. I saw it so clearly in my vision; and the Being that fragmented was my Self . . I saw it. I saw this whole rock fragmented. It all gathered together. When I looked, I am looking at my Self . . a glowing Being like the sun glowing. I've never known that I could . . this little thing talking to you now.

Here every part of the body at my age . . naturally it gets older and parts disappear from it, and yet, I am looking at this Being sitting in a lotus posture and this fantastic beauty. I could hardly believe I could ever in Eternity equal that beauty! And yet I am looking at my Self! And here, this is His meditative world fragmented, and then it is all put back together, and I am looking at my Self. I can't tell you my thrill when I looked at it.

It was first a rock, and then the rock became fragmented. Then the rock was gathered together; but instead of being a rock, it's now a being . . a human being sitting in the lotus posture, meditating. And it's a glorious, beautiful being. I can't describe the beauty of that man; I'm looking at my Self! How can I ever be described as a man called Neville with such beauty? And yet, I am looking at my Self. Such majesty! Such strength of character, such power . . all woven into one being sitting in the lotus posture. And it glows and glows like a sun, and when it reaches the intensity of Power, it explodes. And then I awake here sitting in my apartment on 75th Street in New York City. That's why I am telling you what I know, what I've seen, what I have experienced. But that is true of everyone. You . . there is a Being in you that is meditating you. And the Being in you and the Being in me and the Being in all . . woven together . . form that Being that is the Ultimate God. And that Being is perfect. And may I tell you, I don't care what you've gone through . . you could lose your eyes, lose your hands, lose your feet, be dishonored in this world, but that Being that is meditating you is the most glorious Being you could ever conceive. You have never known such beauty.

Oh, you can go to all the beauty parlors in the world, and they will bring you out and you will think, "Oh, isn't that lovely!" May I tell you, it's just like nothing compared to this Living Being that is meditating you. And that Living Being, and everyone's Living Being all united into one Being, forms the God that fell and fragmented Itself. And each fragment was perfect, and each fragment was the Father of the One meditating that one.

So, I tell you, try it here on this level. There is nothing in this world but God. This greatest of all confessions: "Hear, O Israel, the Lord our God, the Lord is one" . . that there aren't two of us . . not really, in the true sense of the word. But here, you take my word and test it here on this level in the world of Caesar. You want a better future? All right. Dare to take this statement and try it, but try it for this one week.

"I have assumed that I AM the one that I want to be. I AM still assuming that I AM it, and I will continue to assume that I AM it until that which I have assumed is objectively realized" . . and don't give it any time on this level. Just bear down on it, and dare to sleep in that assumption just as though it were true. Don't give it any time.

There is a time limit in what God, your own wonderful Father Who is in the depth of your own Being dreaming you . . He has that time limit; but on this level, there should not be lengths of time. You are told in Paul's letter to the Philippians:

"He who began a good work in you will bring it to completion at the day of Jesus Christ."

All right . . that will take its own good time. You will be brought to the same perfection of the Being who is dreaming you. It is God dreaming Himself into a greater expansion of Himself. That's all that it is. You are the Dreamer and the dream! You are not "another." You are the Dreamer and the dream. "He who began a good work in you will bring it to completion at the day of Jesus Christ." You'll find that in the 1st chapter, the 6th verse, of Philippians. So, you are the Dreamer, dreaming yourself into the image of your Self. That's perfectly all right.

But while you are here, then take it in the world of Caesar and bring about these changes in your world for yourself and for those you love. Eventually you will love all, but if you don't love all now, do it at least for those that you do love, and actually assume it, and dare to say to yourself, "I have assumed it. I AM still assuming it. I will continue to assume it until what I have assumed, and still am assuming, is perfectly realized." For you are told, "Unless you believe that I AM He, you will die in your sins." Is someone talking to me? No. I am saying to myself, "Unless I believe I AM the Being I want to be, I die in my sins. I miss the mark." It's not another talking to me; there is only one God. There can't be two. And so, unless I believe I am that man that I want to be, then I remain as the man that I don't want to be; and therefore I "die in my sins." That is the story as told us in the 8th chapter of the book of John.

It's not another being telling me I must believe in him. Believe in what? I am not called upon to believe in any other being, for any other being is a false god. There's only one God. So, to believe in another . . I don't care who the other appears to be . . to believe in someone who calls himself the head of some great religious body . . whether it be Roman Catholicism, whether it be called Protestantism, whether it be called Judaism . . and to believe that he is the great leader, why, that's a false god. Unless I believe I AM He, I die in my sins. But I don't say that unless I believe that someone is talking to me who tells me unless I believe that he is something . . nonsense! That's all stupid. I don't believe that anyone else is. I must believe that God actually became me, that I may become God!

And so, His name is I AM. So, unless I believe that I am the man that I want to be, then I remain not being that man, and therefore die in my frustration . . and die in my sins. You get it? Sure you do.

So here, I tell you, try it. It may seem difficult, but it will not be difficult if you dare to "go out on a limb" and try it. You are this Being! There is only God. There is nothing but God. Let no one tell you that he is better than you are. There is no one in this world greater than you are! And if anyone dares to tell you that he is, turn your back on him and walk away. I don't care who he is . . or she is . . or they are. There is no one that is your superior, because you are God, and there is nothing but God in this world and God became you, that you may become God.

So, I admire the great, inspired poets. I do! I take Shakespeare and I read him and think, "Isn't this marvelous?" I take Blake. I can't quite follow the arguments of an Einstein . . no. But here are inspired men . . all of them: the Shakespeares, the Blakes, the Einsteins, and all the great painters in the world. But let no one tell you that these inspired men have some influx of Spirit that in any way whatsoever was greater than their own wonderful human imagination, because there is nothing greater than their own human imagination. It didn't come from something outside of themselves; it was their own imagination awakening. "And that same imagination is yours, because there is only one Spirit. There aren't two spirits.

So, the Spirit of Man is one with the Spirit of the Universe that sustains the whole vast world. That's the One Spirit. So, let no one tell you for one moment there is another spirit. There is no other spirit. So, tonight when you go home . . in fact, before you go, start it right here . . and this lovely, wonderful feeling. And may I tell you, I can't tell you what a joy it is to sleep in the assumption . . in the feeling . . that "I AM He."

All right, what comes in the course of the night . . what does it matter? May I tell you, when you slip into the deep, you come hurtling through all kinds of things between the depths of unconsciousness from this level and then waking; and in that one short interval you can have numberless crazy little dreams between the hurtling back from unconsciousness to this level. And you give importance to the little dream, based upon the surface as you are coming through. But you do not know what depths you reach in what is unconscious relative to this level.

So, let no one frighten you. You are an Immortal Being. You cannot die. You just cannot die! And if someone today has arrived at a certain point where it is seemingly before you did, it doesn't matter. He or she . . they are no better because they got there first. There is no "first." Everyone is coming into that level and when all . . and if they don't all come in, may I tell you, it isn't finished. And when all come in, the whole race is over. And what a rejoicing among all who formed the one Body! We are that Body . . that one spirit, that one body, that one lord, that one God and Father of all. There is nothing but God the Father. And everyone will prove to himself by the vision he is God the Father, and he does not resent anyone else being God the Father. How could he?

When Benny came home on Saturday, I can't tell you my thrill. Here is Benny . . and put us together. Let us put Benny on the stage right now. Our pigments are just as opposite as they can be, and we are the same Father of the same Child! I said, "Benny, tell me, what did he look like?" because we have fun together. It's not because we have martinis together. That comes, regardless. It was not because of any martinis. And I said, "Benny, what did he look like?"

He said, "Neville, he was the sweetest blonde . . this blue-eyed, blonde, fair-skinned lad, and here is my Son, and he is calling me 'Father,' and I knew I'm his father. And I so loved him . . I didn't care if the others left me, and left me with all these children. They are all my children anyway. I felt I was the father of all of them, but here was my Special One. Here was David!"

That's the same David that is my Son. Well now, he is the father of my son. Well, if he's the father of my son, are we not one? We are one! But on the surface, this strange, peculiar thing will be fighting each other because he is of a very, very dark skin and I am of an olive skin. Then people think, "Well, my god, they are different!" And it isn't so! In the depths of our Soul, we are one, because God is one. God is not multiple, He is made up of the many, but God is one.

And when he tells me exactly how it happened, the thrill that is mine to see that he and I are one . . and he has the same child! That was the symbol of his "birth from above."

So, may I tell you? Go on. On this level of Caesar, apply this principle. Cushion yourself against the normal blows of the world. It's only natural. You want to be cushioned. You have a wife, a husband, children, friends who cannot cushion themselves because they don't believe it. But you love them to the point where you want to cushion them, regardless of whether they believe it or not.

So, they don't believe it. All right, then you cushion them anyway, because you love them. And you want to leave them enough money to give them a cushion. You aren't going to stop the depth of their own being from giving them blows, but you did your part in so loving them that you want to leave them a cushion. If you want to leave them a cushion in the world of Caesar, you leave them a little money; that's the cushion in this world.

So, what would it feel like if I could leave to those that I so love, say, a hundred thousand . . two hundred thousand? Now, what would it be like to depart this night just as though it meant nothing, and to leave them a quarter of a million, knowing that by tomorrow they may lose the whole thing? But that doesn't really matter. You did your part. You cushioned them for a moment, because the depth of their own being . . which is your own depth . . will simply take them through certain experiences to awaken them to the point where they are the Father of the one and only begotten Son of God. For all are searching for that one Son, to reveal to them the Cause of the phenomena, and the Cause is the Father, for the Father is one's Self.

Then one discovers, "Lord! I AM the only cause of the things that are happening to me in this world? There is not a thing in this world that has ever happened to me that I didn't cause it!" Well, what a responsibility! You mean I caused all the nonsense? Yes, I did. I mean, all the stupid things that happen to me? The blows? Yes. Well, then I've got to stop this peculiar silliness in my world!

Now, let's go into the Silence.

Lecture 3 of 4

You Dare To Assume . . 06-19-1970

Spiritual growth is a gradual transition from a God of tradition to a God of experience. In Blake's works . . one of his letters, rather (23 August 1799) . . he had this little difference of opinion with the Dr. Reverend Trusler; and Trusler said to him, "You need someone to elucidate your ideas."

Blake wrote him a letter saying, "You ought to know that what can be made explicit to the idiot is not worth my care. The wisest of the Ancients discovered that that which was not too explicit was fittest for instruction, because it rouses the faculties to act." Then he asked the Reverend, "Why is it that the Bible is the most instructive work in this world?" Then he answered the Reverend himself, "Is it not because it is addressed to the Imagination, and only immediately to the understanding or reason?"

Well, the Bible is addressed to the Reality of man, for the true identity of man is Jesus Christ; and Jesus Christ is the human imagination! That is the Lord Jesus Christ. "By him all things were made and without Him was not anything made that is made." [John 1:3] And that is the Creator of the world.

Now we will turn to the 17th chapter of the Book of Acts, and you will find a story that is not spelled out because, as Blake said, it is addressed to the imagination. Dig it out. So, Paul addresses the Athenians, and he said, "O men of Athens," . . and then he compliments them on their religious devotions; but then he added, "But as I passed by, I observed over one of your altars this inscription: TO AN UNKNOWN GOD." Then said he to the Athenians, "What, therefore, you worship as unknown, this I proclaim to you: The God who created the world and everything within it is not far off from each one of us. It is in Him that we live, and move, and have our being." [Acts 17:22, 23, 27, 28]

Now you've got to dig it. Start asking questions. I live in Him. I move in Him, and I have my being in Him, and He created the world and everything within it. Blake said,

"I AM not a God afar off. I AM a brother and Friend; Within your own bosoms I reside, and you reside in me," But the perturbed Man, away turned down the valleys dark,"

[from "Jerusalem"]

. . couldn't take it. . . Well, I am going to go a little bit beyond that. I will say that God is not far off; in fact, He is never so far off as even to be near, because nearness implies separation. So, He's not even so far off as even to be near. He became . . actually became . . as we are. His name is I AM. Can you speak of yourself when you say, "I AM," and point elsewhere?

In a dream. who is dreaming? I AM. In a vision, who is having the vision? I AM. In the prison, who is imprisoned? I AM. And who is set free? I AM.

You can't get away from it. So He can never be so far off as even to be near, for nearness implies separation.

This is the God of Whom Paul spoke when he addressed the Athenians, "O men of Athens," . . he praised them, yes, for all their wonderful devotions . . religious devotions. Then he brought up the point, "But as I passed by, I observed this inscription over one of your altars, TO AN UNKNOWN GOD. What, therefore, you worship as unknown, this I proclaim to thee.... The God who created the world and everything within it is not so far off from each one of us, for in Him we live and move and have our being."

That God is your own wonderful human imagination. That's the God of the Universe. One day you will know it. But you are keyed low for Divine purposes, so you don't know it, and you are having this strange, strange, wonderful dream. And this is the dream, but who is dreaming? I am dreaming. One day you will awaken in that immortal head of yours, where the whole drama started and where it comes to an end; and you will discover that you really are the God who created the universe and all within it! But while you are on this level, you can test it and see if this thing is really true.

You mean, my own wonderful human imagination is God! And He, and He alone, creates everything in this world?

I answer, yes. I can't persuade you, I can only suggest that you try it. For, we are told that, "Do you not realize that Jesus Christ is in you? Test Him and see."

Well, how would I test him? Well, tell me Who-He-Is. He is your own wonderful human imagination.

So what? And He created everything in the world, and creates all that is being created, and will continue to create everything that will ever come into the world. And there is no other Creator! And He is in you . . not near, He is your very Being, your own wonderful human imagination!

Well, how do I go about testing this? Well, I simply ignore all the facts of life . . all that reason dictates all that my senses dictate, and I dare to assume that I am the man . . or the woman . . that I want to be. So, I no longer want to be it. I AM it! And I walk in the assumption that I AM it. Then I command, by that assumption, the whole vast world to obey my will.

"I have found . . "What have you found? "I have found in David, the son of Jesse," . . the word "Jesse" is "I AM" . . "I have found in David, the son of Jesse, a man after my own heart, who will do all my will."

Now, who is this being? David is the symbol of humanity. Humanity must obey my will. I don't have to ask them anything. Ask no man, no woman, ask no one. You dare to assume that you are that which you want to be, and David, which is the symbol of humanity, will execute your will.

In the end, when you come to the very end of the drama . . but not before, humanity is gathered together into a single being . . one single unit, and he stands before you, and his name is David. And he calls you "Father."

"I will tell of the decree of the Lord. He said unto me, Thou art my son. Today I have begotten thee." Read that in the Second Psalm. This is David speaking.

Now David says, in the 40th Psalm, "I delight to do Thy will, my God."

If you know Who-You-Are, humanity delights to do your will. So, you dare to assume . . I don't care what it is, it's your privilege to assume good, bad, or indifferent. For He said, "I kill, and I make alive, I wound and I heal. And there is none that can deliver out of my hands." [Deuteronomy 32:39]

If there is only one Creator, don't tell me that He does not also kill! Because who is it then killing? Well, that's a creative act! And who heals? Who wounds, that it may be healed? There is only one God.

"Hear, O Israel, the Lord our God, the Lord is one."

Find out Who-He-Is. I tell you Who-He-Is. He is your own wonderful human imagination. There is no other God. But God lowered Himself down to the limit of man . . the limit of contraction, the limit of opacity . . that he may, in this state of complete oblivion to Who he really is, burst it and start expanding beyond what He was prior to the decision to come down into this state. This is how God expands. He expands and expands and expands. So, He comes down into this state by assuming the limit that is man.

You are man. Well, He never left His name, for He and His name are one! And His name forever is I AM. "This is my name forever and forever, and by this name I shall be known throughout all generations. Go tell them this is my name. I AM hath sent you."

So I say, I AM has sent you. Well, does it make sense? You dwell upon it. It does make sense! And the day will come, you will find the one who has had the experience before you yourself have the experience and you will see him radiating the Glory of God. No questions about it . . you will!

But he could never explain it to anyone who does not have the eyes to see it. Many of you will see it. I have told you what I know from my own experience; and when my time is up and I depart this life, those who have eyes to see it will see and know the quality of the message that I am giving to the world.

I am telling you, there is no other God. Don't look at the speaker. Look at yourself! We are one. I dwell in you, and you dwell in me; and we are one.

I know Who-I-Am. For I have experienced it; but I am not greater than any being in this world. They are only now asleep to the Being that they really are. In the end, we are all one grand brotherhood. And the brotherhood of God forms God, for the God of the Scripture is a compound unity . . one made up of others. We are the "gods," we are the brothers. All came down and assumed these limitations; and the day will come, these woven "garments" that we "wear" we will split from top to bottom; and we who are trapped within them will be set free.

So they said to him, "Is this not Jesus, the son of Joseph? And do we not know his father and mother? And how is it that he now says, I have come down from heaven?"

Here is the perfect example of what happens in everyone when he follows the pattern as described in Scripture. He has everything and experiences everything within himself that is called the "events of the Lord Jesus Christ." And because there is only one Lord Jesus Christ, when he experiences that within himself, he is the Lord Jesus Christ!

But how can he tell it to any one? They will turn their backs upon him as arrogant, as insane, as mad. But he simply tells it, and he knows that everyone who has the eyes to see it can see it now or when he departs this world; and soon after he departs the world, they will have eyes. Eyes will open, and they will see it. There is only one Being, there's only one God, there's only one Lord in the world! Nothing but God!

But here, in the world of Caesar, we can test it. So you want more money? You want a better job? You want an increase in position? Well, assume that you are it now. Don't wait for it. Don't read the papers and have them deny that these things are possible, for today everything is denied.

A little thing that just happened in England: They were so complacent, so sure, they didn't even go to the polls to vote; so Mr. Heath got in. I wondered who was pulling and "treading in the wine press." I wondered who was pulling and "treading in the wine press." I wondered who started the rumor in England that they were so "in" you didn't have to vote. It could be Mr. Heath himself! But it's all imagination.

You suggest, and they accept the suggestions; and then you, knowing they are going to act upon it, go out and then you do exactly what you have to do: work under compulsion to meet everyone you can and get them out. And then he sits back with his pipe, and he is so stunned! He can't believe for one moment they would throw him out, any more than Churchill could believe they would throw him out after the victorious campaign in Europe. But they did!

Everything in this world is possible. Do not say "No" to anything if you want it to be "Yes." Don't give up. Everything is possible, because David does your will, and David is the symbol of humanity. Humanity does your will.

In the end, when you have played all the parts, then David stands before you, not as a group . . as a single youth: this heavenly, heavenly, beautiful being; and you look at him, and he calls you "Father," and you know it. Your memory has returned!

It's all the returning of memory. It was your glory "before that the world" started. And you will say these words in the

17 chapter of the Book of John: "I have accomplished the work you sent me to do. Now return unto me the glory that was mine, the glory that I had with Thee before that the world was." [John 17:5]

He seems to be speaking of another, but the Being "sent" and the Sender are one. And the Being "sent" is not inferior in his Essential Being, but only as to the office of the One that is "sent." So, he is sent into the world. So while he is in the world as the one who is "sent," his office is inferior to the Sender who does not leave that stable state. But he, the "sent," and the Sender are one!

So "He who sees me sees Him who sent me."

So you will see me with your incurrent eyes, and see me playing the part described in Scripture. I don't have to pretend. Neville . . yes . . a little, tiny man, meaning nothing in the world socially, financially, intellectually, or in any other manner . . nothing, but it doesn't matter. I willed to play this part. Only through this part could I tell the story, and tell it so that unnumbered generations from now it will be told and retold, but magnified. For those now living will be eye witnesses to the event before the departure of the little garment. They will be eye witnesses to the story. For all you have to do is to go into the Bible, and there you will see the story. And if within current eyes you see him playing the parts recorded in Scripture two thousand years ago, then you know Who-He-Is. But I am not alone! Everyone is going to play this part, for there is only God. He is not playing the part as one little being set aside . . no, He is not far off. He is not even near, for nearness implies separation. "God actually became as we are, that we maybe as He is." [Blake, from "There Is No Natural Religion"]

So when you imagine something, remember: It is God Acting! And God's actions are His words. "And His word cannot return unto Him void but it must accomplish that which He purposed, and prosper in the thing for which He sent it."

Well, what are you imagining? Whatever you are imagining, you are actually sending into being to be confronted with it. So if you really want a lovely life, be careful what you are imagining, because imagination is God. Imagining is God-in-action! So what are you imagining? That everything is going down? That the whole world is collapsing? Well then, if that is what you imagine, may I tell you? You will have the experience of a collapsed world, but others won't.

There are people today making fortunes out of the seeming collapsed market . . fortunes, they are making! They held their cash. I read in the New York Times of last Sunday [June 14] . . I get the Sunday issue every week, and it came a little late this week. In the financial section this house . . not one of the biggest houses, but a good house . . and they are in the "black," they never once went into the "red." And the man's name is Gardener, and they are quoting him. He said, "In 1968, in the summer of '68, we knew this was coming, and we prepared for the recession. So we were not caught in it. We knew and prepared for it, for it had to come."

Well, that was an imaginal act. He was bringing it about within himself because he knew it had to come. It wasn't going to come in spite of someone imagining that it had to come. And so, he planned it within his own mind's eye. So then came 1970 and then came the radical, radical decline. They had cash; they could pick up all these things at the bottom. They've got to go back. This is a powerful land, for you and I are imaginative people.

Americans went to the moon. That's imagination. They will go to everything in this world that they want to go to, for this is a fabulous land. Well, you can't stop men imagining, and we do imagine in this country! We build the tallest . . build all kinds of things because man here . . you can't stop it. He is so constructed, he imagines all the time.

Well, you can't stop it going back; so he started the decline in his own mind's eye in the summer of '68, and waited patiently . . waited and waited, and then came the inevitable crash. It will go back. But he had cash; waiting for what he knew was inevitable. So instead of buying it at 900, he now buys it in the 600's. It served him to wait a year and a half or two years, for what would he make now coming in at this bottom, when it starts moving again?

It's all within the imagination of man. But I am not an economist; I know nothing about economy. I am not interested in it. I get calls all the time saying, "Will you go into a business with me?" I am not interested. I got one yesterday. He cried on the phone when I would not come forward to buy a huge, large area of land for him because he wants to be a grower of trees. I said, "I'm not interested. I am not in business. I am telling you a principle and you don't have to turn to anyone in this world to ask their assistance."

The whole vast world will rush to serve you if you assume a certain state and remain faithful to that assumption. If I dare to assume that I am the man that I want to be, the world has to come to my assistance and express it, for the world is David, and David is "a man after my heart who will do all my will."

And in the end, you will see him standing before you, not as humanity, but a single being . . a glorified, glorious boy . . a boy of about 12 or 13 at the most. And, oh! What a beauty he is. The sum total of all of humanity who did your will. So when you played all the parts, then you will know: "I came down from Heaven." . . And they will say, "But I know your parents. I know your father and your mother."

Yes, they know my parents of the "garment" that I "wear," and they know my brothers and my sister, who are brothers and sisters of the "garment" that I "wear." But the wearer of the garment, they do not know. They do not know the Occupant of that garment. For that garment only serves the occupant for a purpose. And in this very moment he has completed the task.

I can say tonight, "I have accomplished the work which Thou sent me to do. Now return the glory that was mine, the glory that I had with Thee before that the world was." And may I tell you? He has, He has! I am not waiting for the return. But the mask hides it from those who have not incurrent eyes to see it. But everyone will see it. Everyone will experience it. But while we are here, you play your part perfectly, not only for yourself; play it for everyone in the world, for they are all "yourself pushed out" anyway.

So someone wants this, that or the other? As I said to my friend . . he cried on the phone. I said, "I am speaking of a principle. I will 'hear' you tell me that you have your whatever acreage you want to plant your avocado pears, if you want to do that for a living, for they grow without effort on your part."

What he really wants . . he doesn't want to do anything. He wants to have something planted that simply produces, like people buying stock. He is not interested in the

Company, only in the little piece of paper, not the Company, what it is doing or the management of the Company. So he wants an area of avocado pears. Even though he doesn't want to work, I will still "hear" that he has it. I am not here to judge anyone in the world. So he wants that? I will "hear" that he has it, and assume that he has it;' and may I tell you? He will have it. For the world will wait on him and the world will see that he has it; and he will never know, as told us in the very first chapter and the second chapter of Isaiah, that it was I who pray for him, because he cried and hung up, he could not wait. But I did not. When he hung up crying, I did not until I had "heard" that he has what he wants.

But I need not be the medium through which he has whatever it takes to buy his "X" number of acres for his plants, because I am not in business. I am simply telling a story . . an eternal story that is true. And the story is all for us in Scripture.

Jesus Christ is the true identity of every child born of woman. And Jesus Christ is the human imagination. "Through Him, all things were made, and without Him was not anything made that was made."

"He is in the world, and the world knows Him not"

So no one knows Him. He sits, and no one knows He is the Cause of the phenomena of life. And they turn to this place, that place, the other place; and here is one "treading out the wine press," knowing exactly what he is doing, allowing his will to express through humanity . . humanity being David, the son of Jesse. And Jesse is I AM. It is any form of the verb "to be." "I AM" . . that's the name of Jesse.

So, "Whose son are you?" "I AM the son of your servant." "Jesse."

And "Now I have found in David, the son of Jesse, a man after my own heart, who will do all my will."

So humanity will do it. Everyone will do it. And in the end, you will awaken, and you will discover that the whole drama started in your immortal head, and in that immortal head you dreamed the Dream of Life. And one day you heard a Voice, it was a wind . . a strange wind, and you awoke from the Dream of Life to discover that you had dreamed it all. You were a dreamer and then you came out, and all the imagery of Scripture surrounds you. Everything about it surrounds you, and you are the One of whom it spoke in Scripture "born not of blood, nor of the will of man, nor of the will of the flesh, but of God." It was God reborn. You are the one destined to be reborn.

Don't let anyone tell you that you began in your mother's womb or that you even began. There never was a time that you and I were not . . never. Nor will there come a time when you and I shall cease to be. Before this whole vast world appeared to be, you and I were the creators of it. I know our scientists will question that and think me mad. It's perfectly all right. I will go along with Blake, based upon my visions.

> "Eternity exists,
> and all things in Eternity,
> Independent of Creation,
> which was an act of mercy."

[From "A Vision of the Last Judgment"]

And then what is that creation? All things exist. Humanity, the animal world, the plant world . . everything exists in Eternity, and Eternity is in your own wonderful human imagination. That's Eternity!

All things exist now in the human imagination. Well now, what is the act of creation that I would bury myself in that which exists and return? That I could "die" . . actually die . . and return? For a seed must fall into the ground and die before it is made alive. If it does not fall into the ground and "die," it remains alone; but if it falls and dies, it brings forth much. So I "died," I fell into my own wonderful world that is . . it exists, and the world is "dead" . . completely dead. And I could not pretend. I had to actually become this world of the "dead." So I became it, and then I passed through all the horrors of the world. For what purpose? To remember the glory that I saw before, that I gave up to come into this world.

"How long, how vast, how severe the anguish 'ere I find that glory were long to tell."

But having gone through it all, then I remembered. And the only one that could actually bring me back to my memory of the glory that was mine was my "son," for "No one knows who the Father is except the Son, and no one knows who the Son is except the Father."

And so here the son stands before me and the memory . . ancient, ancient memory returned. And I was the one who decided without any persuasion to lay myself down.

He said, "No one takes away my life. I lay it down myself. I have the power to lay it down, and the power to lift it up again." But while I lay it down:

"Then those in Great Eternity who contemplate on death Said thus: What seems to be, is to those to whom It seems to Be." [From "Jerusalem"]

Here I AM in a world. It seems that he is going to attack me. I am assuming that? Well then, he will attack me.

I assume that things are going to be bad, they will be bad.

I assume that things are going to break, and I am going to wait for it. So . . "What seems to Be, is, To those to whom It seems to Be, and is productive of the most dreadful Consequences to those to whom it seems to Be, even of Torments, Despair and Eternal Death; but the Divine Mercy Steps beyond and Redeems Man in the Body of Jesus."

So that act of mercy is the act of Creation, when I . . the Eternal Being . . gave up my Eternal Self and came down into a finite world and "died." And the act of creation is the redemptive act when I am brought back, because I am lost in a world where "what seems to be is, to those to whom it seems to be."

And when I have gone through the entire gamut of all the experiences of man, then I hear the Voice. The Voice is the wind . . an unearthly wind; and you hear it within the immortal head where the drama started. And then you find yourself waking, and you awake within yourself, and then you come out of the tomb in which you were entombed. As you come out, the imagery of the birth of God surrounds you, and you are the star in the drama.

And from then on, three great events take place, and it's all over. The Descent of the Dove upon . . the symbol of the Holy Spirit is completely satisfied with the journey, for the journey is now over; and "this is my beloved Son, in whom I AM well pleased." [Matthew 3:17]

One of my sons has returned. When all the sons return, all the sons together from God the Father. We are the Elohim, and together we form Jehovah. But we are the gods . . all of us.

By the way, we got our contract today from the club. They finally came through with a contract. So will be returning the last week of September . . same place, same time.

Now are there any questions, please?

QUESTIONS BY A LADY: Do you have any more understanding as to why we have to leave before some people experience the Power from on high?

NEVILLE: Well, we are told in Scripture: "Remain just where you are until you are clothed with Power from on high." All will be clothed in Power. But not very many . . strangely enough, only the women saw him. All saw him after that, but the women saw him. Why, I do not know. They saw him in his transfigured state. He did take three into the state, but that is "before that the world was." He is not talking of anything in this world.

Everything that is said from the lips of the one called Jesus Christ is of another world . . a world which is his true home, from which he came and to which he will return. But men misunderstood him. For they knew the early man, and they would say, "We know his father. His name is Joseph. We know his father and his mother and his brother and his sisters. How can he tell us, I have come down from heaven?" That's an insane statement for any man to make, but he was never speaking of anything of this world.

After you have the experiences, you will have the same social gathering that you've always had; but in the midst of the most intimate relationships, you know they are only brothers of your body that you "wear." Behind the garments that they wear, they are your eternal brothers; but they do not know that as yet. They know only the physical descent, but they do not know the spiritual beings that they are. So if you told them that you are the father of David of Biblical fame, they would be concerned and think, "We had better take good care of him, because he's not all here." So you don't tell them.

But in the midst of the gathering, you know Who-You-Are, and they don't know Who. . You-Are; and so as you walk the street, you walk in the consciousness of being the Father of the Son of God.

Humanity seems so vast. Three and a half billion, and they are growing; and yet all this did you will through the centuries, that you dreamed the Dream of Life. And in the end, it formed itself into a single youth who called you "Father." So you walk in that consciousness.

If you could only get the accustomed aspect of things out of your eyes and drop in on yourselves as strangers, just like some visitor from Heaven! Here I drop in on myself, but Neville belongs to a certain family physically in this world; and then after the experience you get the accustomed aspect of things out of your eyes; and you walk not as the brother of this large, wonderful family of physical descent but you walk in the consciousness of being the Father of the Son of God!

Let us go into the Silence.

Lecture 4 of 4

Radio Talk - The Law of Assumption

Station KECA, Los Angeles
July, 1951

The great mystic, William Blake, wrote almost two hundred years ago,

"What seems to be, is, to those to whom it seems to be and is productive of the most dreadful consequences to those to whom it seems to be."

Now, at first, this mystical gem seems a bit involved, or at best to be a play on words; but it is nothing of the kind. Listen to it carefully.

"What seems to be, is, to those to whom it seems to be."

That is certainly clear enough. It is a simple truth about the law of assumption, and a warning of the consequences of its misuse.

The author of the Epistle to the Romans declared in the fourteenth chapter,

"I know, and am persuaded by the Lord Jesus, that there is nothing unclean of itself; but to him that esteemeth anything to be unclean, to him it is unclean."

We see by this that it is not superior insight but purblindness that reads into the greatness of men some littleness with which it chances to be familiar, for what seems to be, is, to those to whom it seems to be.

Experiments recently conducted at two of our leading universities revealed this great truth about the law of assumption.

They stated in their releases to the newspapers, that after two thousand experiments they came to the conclusion that,

'What you see when you look at something depends not so much on what is there as on the assumption you make when you look. What you believe to be the real physical world, is actually only an assumptive world."

In other words, you would not define your husband in the same way that your mother would. Yet, you are both defining the same person.

Your particular relationship to a thing influences your feelings with respect to that thing and makes you see in it an element which is not there.

If your feeling in the matter is a self-element; it can be cast out. If it is a permanent distinction in the state considered, it cannot be cast out.

The thing to do is to try.

If you can change your opinion of another, then what you now believe of him cannot be absolutely true, but relatively true.

Men believe in the reality of the external world because they do not know how to focus and condense their powers to penetrate its thin crust.

Strangely enough, it is not difficult to penetrate this view of the senses.

To remove the veil of the senses, we do not employ great effort; the objective world vanishes as we turn our attention from it.

We have only to concentrate on the state desired to mentally see it; but to give reality to it so that it will become an objective fact, we must focus our attention upon the desired state until it has all the sensory vividness and feeling of reality.

When, through concentrated attention, our desire appears to possess the distinctness and feeling of reality; when the form of thought is as vivid as the form of nature, we have given it the right to become a visible fact in our lives.

Each man must find the means best suited to his nature to control his attention and concentrate it on the desired state.

I find for myself the best state to be one of meditation, a relaxed state akin to sleep, but a state in which I am still consciously in control of my imagination and capable of fixing my attention on a mental object.

If it is difficult to control the direction of your attention while in this state akin to sleep, you may find gazing fixedly into an object very helpful. Do not look at its surface, but rather into and beyond any plain object such as a wall, a carpet or any object which possesses depth. Arrange it to return as little reflection as possible. Imagine, then, that in this depth you are seeing and hearing what you want to see and hear until your attention is exclusively occupied by the imagined state.

At the end of your meditation, when you awake from your controlled waking dream you feel as though you had returned from a great distance.

The visible world which you had shut out, returns to consciousness and, by its very presence, informs you that you have been self-deceived into believing that the object of your contemplation was real; but if you remain faithful to your vision this sustained mental attitude will give reality to your visions and they will become visible concrete facts in your world.

Define your highest ideal and concentrate your attention upon this ideal until you identify yourself with it. Assume the feeling of being it, the feeling that would be yours were you now embodying it in your world.

This assumption, though now denied by your senses,

"if persisted in",

will become a fact in your world. You will know when you have succeeded in fixing the desired state in consciousness simply

by looking mentally at the people you know.

This is a wonderful check on yourself, as your mental conversations are more revealing than your physical conversations are. If, in your mental conversations with others, you talk with them as you formerly did, then you have not changed your concept of self, for all changes of concepts of self result in a changed relationship to the world.

Remember what was said earlier,

"What you see when you look at something depends not so much on what is there as on the assumption you make when you look."

Therefore, the assumption of the wish fulfilled should make you see the world mentally as you would physically were your assumption a physical fact.

The spiritual man speaks to the natural man through the language of desire. The key to progress in life and to the fulfillment of dreams lies in the ready obedience to the voice. Unhesitating obedience to its voice is an immediate assumption of the wish fulfilled.

To desire a state is to have it.

As Pascal said,

"You would not have sought me
had you not already found me."

Man, by assuming the feeling of the wish fulfilled and then living and acting on this conviction changes his future in harmony with his assumption.

To "change his future" is the inalienable right of freedom loving individuals. There would be no progress in the world were it not for the divine discontent in man which urges him on to higher and higher levels of consciousness.

I have chosen this subject so close to the hearts of us all . . "Changing Your Future" . . for my message next Sunday morning. I am to have the great joy of speaking for Dr. Bailes while he is vacationing. The service will be held at 10:30 at the Fox Wilshire Theater on Wilshire Boulevard near La Cienega Boulevard. Since the right to change our future is our birthright as sons of God, let us accept its challenge and learn just how to do it.

Again today, speaking of changing your future, I wish to stress the importance of a real transformation of self . . not merely a slight alteration of circumstances which, in a matter of moments, will permit us to slip back into the old dissatisfied man.

In your meditation, allow others to see you as they would see you were this new concept of self a concrete fact. You always seem to others the embodiment of the ideal you inspire. Therefore, in meditation, when you contemplate others, you must be seen by them mentally as you would be seen by them physically were your conception of yourself an objective fact.

That is, in meditation, you imagine that they see you expressing this nobler man you desire to be. If you assume that you are what you want to be, your desire is fulfilled and, in fulfillment, all longing "to be" is neutralized.

This, also, is an excellent check on yourself as to whether or not you have actually succeeded in changing self. You cannot continue desiring what has been realized. Rather, you are in a mood to give thanks for a gift received.

Your desire is not something you labor to fulfill, it is recognizing something you already possess. It is assuming the feeling of being that which you desire to be.

Believing and being are one. The conceiver and his conception are one. Therefore, that which you conceive yourself to be can never be so far off as even to be near, for nearness implies separation.

> "If thou canst believe, all things
> are possible to him that believeth."

Faith is the substance of things hoped for, the evidence of things not yet seen.

If you assume that you are that finer, nobler one you wish to be, you will see others as they are related to your high assumption.

All enlightened men wish for the good of others.

If it is the good of another you seek, you must use the same controlled contemplation.

In meditation, you must represent the other to yourself as already being or having the greatness you desire for him. As for yourself, your desire for another must be an intense one. It is through desire that you rise above your present sphere and the road from longing, to fulfillment, is shortened, as you experience in imagination, all that you would experience in the flesh, were you or your friend the embodiment of the desire you have for yourself or him.

Experience has taught me that this is the perfect way to achieve my great goals for others as well as for myself.

However, my own failures would convict me were I to imply that I have completely mastered the control of my attention.

I can, however, with the ancient teacher say:

"This one thing I do, forgetting those things which are behind, and reaching forth unto those things which are before . . I press towards the mark for the prize."

NEVILLE'S CASE HISTORIES, from The Power of Awareness, citing examples on the use of the Law of Assumption.

CASE HISTORY 1

This is a story with every detail of which I am personally familiar.

In the spring of 1943, a recently drafted soldier was stationed in a large army camp in Louisiana. He was intensely eager to get out of the army, but only in an entirely honorable way.

The only way he could do this was to apply for a discharge. The application then required the approval of his commanding officer to become effective. Based on army regulations, the decision of the commanding officer was final and could not be appealed. The soldier, following all the necessary procedure, applied for a discharge. Within four hours, this application was returned . . marked "disapproved". Convinced he could not appeal the decision to any higher authority, military or civilian, he turned within to his own consciousness, determined to rely on the law of assumption.

The soldier realized that his consciousness was the only reality, that his particular state of consciousness determined the events he would encounter.

That night, in the interval between getting into bed and falling asleep, he concentrated on consciously using the law of assumption. In imagination, he felt himself to be in his own apartment in New York City. He visualized his apartment, that is, in his mind's eye he actually saw his own apartment, mentally picturing each one of the familiar rooms with all the furnishings vividly real.

With this picture clearly visualized, and lying flat on his back, he completely relaxed physically. In this way, he induced a state bordering on sleep, at the same time retaining control of the direction of his attention. When his body was completely immobilized, he assumed that he was in his own room and felt himself to be lying in his own bed .. a very different feeling from that of lying on an army cot.

In imagination, he rose from the bed, walked from room to room, touching various pieces of furniture. He then went to the window and, with his hands resting on the sill, looked out on the street on which his apartment faced. So vivid was all this in his imagination that he saw in detail the pavement, the railings, the trees and the familiar red brick of the building on the opposite side of the street. He then returned to his bed and felt himself drifting off to sleep.

He knew that it was most important in the successful use of this law that at the actual point of falling asleep, his consciousness be filled with the assumption that he was already what he wanted to be. All that he did in imagination was based on the assumption that he was no longer in the army. Night after night, the soldier enacted this drama. Night after night, in imagination, he felt himself, honorably discharged, back in his home, seeing all the familiar surroundings and falling asleep in his own bed. This continued for eight nights.

For eight days, his objective experience continued to be directly opposite to his subjective experience in consciousness each night, before going to sleep. On the ninth day, orders came through from Battalion headquarters for the soldier to fill out a new application for his discharge. Shortly after this was done, he was ordered to report to the Colonel's office. During the discussion, the Colonel asked him if he was still desirous of getting out of the army. Upon receiving an affirmative reply, the Colonel said that he personally disagreed, and while he had strong objections to approving of the discharge, he had decided to overlook these objections and to approve it. Within a few hours, the application was approved and the soldier, now a civilian, was on a train bound for home.

Case History 2

This is a striking story of an extremely successful businessman demonstrating the power of imagination and the law of assumption.

I know this family intimately, and all the details were told to me by the son described herein.

The story begins when he was twenty years old.

He was next to the oldest in a large family of nine brothers and one sister. The father was one of the partners in a small merchandising business. In his eighteenth year, the brother referred to in this story left the country in which they lived and traveled two thousand miles to enter college and complete his education.

Shortly after his first year in college, he was called home because of a tragic event in connection with his father's business. Through the machinations of his associates, the father was not only forced out of his business, but was the object of false accusations impugning his character and integrity.

At the same time, he was deprived of his rightful share in the equity of the business. The result was he found himself largely discredited and almost penniless. It was under these circumstances that the son was called home from college.

He returned, his heart filled with one great resolution. He was determined that he would become outstandingly successful in business. The first thing he and his father did was to use the little money they had to start their own business. They rented a small store on a side street not far from the large business of which the father had been one of the principal owners. There they started a business bent upon real service to the community. It was shortly thereafter that the son, with instinctive awareness that it was bound to work, deliberately used imagination to attain an almost fantastic objective.

Every day, on the way to and from work, he passed the building of his father's former business, the biggest business of its kind in the country. It was one of the largest buildings, with the most prominent location in the heart of the city. On the outside of the building was a huge sign on which the name of the firm was painted in large bold letters.

Day after day, as he passed by, a great dream took shape in the son's mind. He thought of how wonderful it would be if it was his family that had this great building . . his family that owned and operated this great business.

One day, as he stood gazing at the building, in his imagination, he saw a completely different name on the huge sign across the entrance. Now the large letters spelled out his family name (in these case histories actual names are not used; for the sake of clarity, in this story we will use hypothetical names and assume that the son's family name was Lordard).

Where the sign read F. N. Moth & Co., in imagination, he actually saw the name, letter by letter, N. Lordard & Sons.

He remained looking at the sign with his eyes wide open, imagining that it read N. Lordard & Sons. Twice a day, week after week, month after month, for two years, he saw his family name over the front of that building. He was convinced that if he felt strongly enough that a thing was true, it was bound to be the case, and by seeing in imagination his family name on the sign, which implied that they owned the business, he became convinced that one day they would own it.

During this period, he told only one person what he was doing. He confided in his mother, who with loving concern tried to discourage him in order to protect him from what might be a great disappointment.

Despite this, he persisted day after day.

Two years later, the large company failed and the coveted building was up for sale.

On the day of the sale, he seemed no nearer ownership than he had been two years before when he began to apply the law of assumption.

During this period, they had worked hard, and their customers had implicit confidence in them. However, they had not earned anything like the amount of money required for the purchase of the property. Nor did they have any source from which they could borrow the necessary capital. Making even more remote their chance of getting it was the fact that this was regarded as the most desirable property in the city and a number of wealthy business people were prepared to buy it.

On the actual day of the sale, to their complete surprise, a man, almost a total stranger, came into their shop and offered to buy the property for them. (Due to some unusual conditions involved in this transaction, the son's family could not even make a bid for the property.)

They thought the man was joking. However, this was not the case. The man explained that he had watched them for some time, admired their ability, believed in their integrity, and that supplying the capital for them to go into business on a large scale was an extremely sound investment for him. That very day the property was theirs. What the son had persisted in seeing in his imagination was now a reality. The hunch of the stranger was more than justified.

Today, this family owns not only the particular business referred to, but owns many of the largest industries in the country in which they live.

The son, seeing his family name over the entrance of this great building, long before it was actually there, was using exactly the technique that produces results.

By assuming the feeling that he already had what he desired, by making this a vivid reality in his imagination, by determined persistence, regardless of appearance or circumstance, he inevitably caused his dream to become a reality.

CASE HISTORY 3

This is the story of a very unexpected result of an interview with a lady who came to consult me.

One afternoon, a young grandmother, a businesswoman in New York, came to see me. She brought along her nine-year-old grandson, who was visiting her from his home in Pennsylvania.

In response to her questions, I explained the law of assumption, describing in detail the procedure to be followed in attaining an objective. The boy sat quietly, apparently absorbed in a small toy truck, while I explained to the grandmother the method of assuming the state of consciousness that would be hers were her desire already fulfilled. I told her the story of the soldier in camp, who, each night, fell asleep, imagining himself to be in his own bed in his own home.

When the boy and his grandmother were leaving, he looked up at me with great excitement and said, "I know what I want and, now, I know how to get it". Surprised, I asked him what it was he wanted; he told me he had his heart set on a puppy.

To this, the grandmother vigorously protested, telling the boy that it had been made clear repeatedly that he could not have a dog under any circumstances... that his father and mother would not allow it, that the boy was too young to care for it properly, and furthermore, the father had a deep dislike for dogs . . he actually hated to have one around.

All these were arguments the boy, passionately desirous of having a dog, refused to understand.

"Now I know what to do", he said. "Every night, just as I am going off to sleep, I am going to pretend that I have a dog and we are going for a walk". "No", said the grandmother, "that is not what Mr. Neville means. This was not meant for you. You cannot have a dog".

Approximately six weeks later, the grandmother told me what was to her an astonishing story.

The boy's desire to own a dog was so intense that he had absorbed all that I had told his grandmother of how to attain one's desire . . and he believed implicitly that at last he knew how to get a dog. Putting this belief into practice, for many nights, the boy imagined a dog was lying in his bed beside him. In imagination, he petted the dog, actually feeling its fur. Things like playing with the dog and taking it for a walk filled his mind.

Within a few weeks, it happened. A newspaper in the city in which the boy lived organized a special program in connection with Kindness to Animals Week. All school children were requested to write an essay on "Why I Would Like to Own a Dog".

After entries from all the schools were submitted and judged, the winner of the contest was announced. The very same boy who weeks before in my apartment in New York had told me "Now I know how to get a dog" was the winner. In an elaborate ceremony, which was publicized with stories and pictures in the newspaper, the boy was awarded a beautiful collie puppy.

In relating this story, the grandmother told me that if the boy had been given the money with which to buy a dog, the parents would have refused to do so and would have used it to buy a bond for the boy or put it in the savings bank for him.

Furthermore, if someone had made the boy a gift of a dog, they would have refused it or given it away. But the dramatic manner in which they boy got the dog, the way he won the city-wide contest, the stories and pictures in the newspaper, the pride of achievement and joy of the boy himself all combined to bring about a change of heart in the parents, and they found themselves doing that which they never conceived possible . . they allowed him to keep the dog.

All this the grandmother explained to me, and she concluded by saying that there was one particular kind of dog on which the boy had set his heart. It was a collie.

CASE HISTORY 4

This was told by the aunt in the story to the entire audience at the conclusion of one of my lectures.

During the question period following my lecture on the law of assumption, a lady who had attended many lectures and had had personal consultation with me on a number of occasions, rose and asked permission to tell a story illustrating how she had successfully used the law.

She said that upon returning home from the lecture the week before, she had found her niece distressed and terribly upset. The husband of the niece, who was an officer in the Army Air Force stationed in Atlantic City, had just been ordered, along with the rest of his unit, to active duty in Europe. She tearfully told her aunt that the reason she was upset was that she had been hoping her husband would be assigned to Florida as an Instructor. They both loved Florida and were anxious to be stationed there and not to be separated.

Upon hearing this story, the aunt stated that there was only one thing to do and that was to apply immediately the law of assumption. "Let's actualize it", she said. "If you were actually in Florida, what would you do? You would feel the warm breeze. You would smell the salt air. You would feel your toes sinking down into the sand. Well, let's do all that right now".

They took off their shoes and, turning out the lights, in imagination, they felt themselves actually in Florida, feeling the warm breeze, smelling the sea air, pushing their toes into the sand.

Forty-eight hours later, the husband received a change of orders. His new instructions were to report immediately to Florida as an Air Force Instructor. Five days later, his wife was on a train to join him.

While the aunt, in order to help her niece to attain her desire, joined in with the niece in assuming the state of consciousness required, she did not go to Florida. That was not her desire. On the other hand, that was the intense longing of the niece.

Case History 5

This case is especially interesting because of the short interval of time between the application of this law of assumption and its visible manifestation.

A very prominent woman came to me in deep concern. She maintained a lovely city apartment and a large country home; but because the many demands made upon her were greater than her modest income, it was absolutely essential that she rent her apartment if she and her family were to spend the summer at their country home.

In previous years, the apartment had been rented without difficulty early in the spring, but the day she came to me, the rental season for summer sublets was over. The apartment had been in the hands of the best real estate agents for months, but no one had been interested even in coming to see it.

When she had described her predicament, I explained how the law of assumption could be brought to bear on solving her problem. I suggested that, by imagining the apartment had been rented by a person desiring immediate occupancy and by assuming that this was the case, her apartment actually would be rented.

In order to create the necessary feeling of naturalness, the feeling that it was already a fact that her apartment was rented, I suggested that she drift off into sleep that very night, imagining herself, not in her apartment, but in whatever place she would sleep were the apartment suddenly rented. She quickly grasped the idea and said that in such a situation she would sleep in her country home, even though it was not yet opened for the summer.

This interview took place on Thursday. At nine o'clock the following Saturday morning, she phoned me from her home in the country, excited and happy. She told me that on Thursday night she had fallen asleep actually imagining and feeling that she was sleeping in her other bed in her country home many miles away from the city apartment she was occupying.

On Friday, the very next day, a highly desirable tenant, one who met all her requirements as a responsible person, not only rented the apartment, but rented it on the condition that he could move in that very day.

CASE HISTORY 6

Only the most complete and intense use of the law of assumption could have produced such results in this extreme situation.

Four years ago, a friend of our family asked that I talk with his twenty-eight-year-old son, who was not expected to live.

He was suffering from a rare heart disease. This disease resulted in a disintegration of the organ. Long and costly medical care had been of no avail. Doctors held out no hope for recovery. For a long time, the son had been confined to his bed. His body had shrunk to almost a skeleton, and he could talk and breathe only with great difficulty. His wife and two small children were home when I called, and his wife was present throughout our discussion.

I started by telling him that there was only one solution to any problem, and that solution was a change of attitude.

Since talking exhausted him, I asked him to nod in agreement if he understood clearly what I said. This he agreed to do. I described the facts underlying the law of consciousness . . in fact that consciousness was the only reality. I told him that the way to change any condition was to change his state of consciousness concerning it.

As a specific aid in helping him to assume the feeling of already being well, I suggested that in imagination, he see the doctor's face expressing incredulous amazement in finding him recovered, contrary to all reason, from the last stages of an incurable disease, that he see him double checking in his examination and hear him saying over and over, "It's a miracle . . it's a miracle".

He not only understood all this clearly, but he believed it implicitly. He promised that he would faithfully follow this procedure. His wife, who had been listening intently, assured me that she, too, would diligently use the law of assumption and her imagination in the same way as her husband.

The following day I sailed for New York . . all this taking place during a winter vacation in the tropics.

Several months later, I received a letter saying the son had made a miraculous recovery. On my next visit, I met him in person. He was in perfect health, actively engaged in business and thoroughly enjoying the many social activities of his friends and family.

He told me that from the day I left, he never had any doubt that "it" would work. He described how he had faithfully followed the suggestion I had made to him and day after day had lived completely in the assumption of already being well and strong.

Now, four years after his recovery, he is convinced that the only reason he is here today is due to his successful use of the law of assumption.

CASE HISTORY 7

This story illustrates the successful use of the law by a New York business executive.

In the fall of 1950, an executive of one of New York's prominent banks discussed with me a serious problem with which he was confronted.

He told me that the outlook for his personal progress and advancement was very dim. Having reached middle age and feeling that a marked improvement in position and income was justified, he had "talked it out" with his superiors.

They frankly told him that any major improvement was impossible and intimated that if he was dissatisfied, he could seek another job.

This, of course, only increased his uneasiness. In our talk, he explained that he had no great desire for really big money, but that he had to have a substantial income in order to maintain his home comfortably and to provide for the education of his children in good preparatory schools and colleges. This he found impossible on his present income.

The refusal of the bank to assure him of any advancement in the near future resulted in a feeling of discontent and an intense desire to secure a better position with considerably more money. He confided in me that the kind of job he would like better than anything in the world was one in which he managed the investment funds of a large institution such as a foundation or great university.

In explaining the law of assumption, I stated that his present situation was only a manifestation of his concept of himself and declared that if he wanted to change the circumstances in which he found himself, he could do so by changing his concept of himself.

In order to bring about this change of consciousness, and thereby a change in his situation, I asked him to follow this procedure every night just before he fell asleep:

In imagination, he was to feel he was retiring at the end of one of the most important and successful days of his life. He was to imagine that he had actually closed a deal that very day to join the kind of organization he yearned to be with and in exactly the capacity he wanted.

I suggested to him that if he succeeded in completely filling his mind with this feeling, he would experience a definite sense of relief. In this mood, his uneasiness and discontent would be a thing of the past. He would feel the contentment that comes with the fulfillment of desire. I wound up by assuring him that if he did this faithfully, he would inevitably get the kind of position he wanted.

This was the first week of December. Night after night, without exception, he followed this procedure. Early in February, a director of one of the wealthiest foundations in the world asked this executive if he would be interested in joining the foundation in an executive capacity handling investments. After some brief discussion, he accepted.

Today, at a substantially higher income and with the assurance of steady progress, this man is in a position far exceeding all that he had hoped for.

Case History 8

The man and wife in this story have attended my lectures for a number of years.

It is an interesting illustration of the conscious use of this law by two people concentrating on the same objective at one time.

This man and wife were an exceptionally devoted couple. Their life was completely happy and entirely free from any problems or frustrations.

For some time, they had planned to move into a larger apartment. The more they thought about it, the more they realized that what they had their hearts set on was a beautiful penthouse.

In discussing it together, the husband explained that he wanted one with a huge window looking out on a magnificent view. The wife said she would like to have one side of the walls mirrored from top to bottom. They both wanted to have a wood-burning fireplace.

It was a "must" that the apartment be in New York City.

For months, they had searched for just such an apartment in vain. In fact, the situation in the city was such that the securing of any kind of apartment was almost an impossibility. They were so scarce that not only were there waiting lists for them, but all sorts of special deals including premiums, the buying of furniture etc.., were involved. New apartments were being leased long before they were completed, many being rented from the blueprints of the building.

Early in the spring, after months of fruitless seeking, they finally located one which they seriously considered. It was a penthouse apartment in a building just being completed on upper Fifth Avenue facing Central Park. It had one serious drawback. Being a new building, it was not subject to rent control, and the couple felt the yearly rental was exorbitant. In fact, it was several thousand dollars a year more than they had considered paying.

During the spring months of March and April, they continued looking at various penthouses throughout the city, but they always came back to this one. Finally, they decided to increase the amount they would pay substantially and made a proposition which the agent for the building agreed to forward to the owners for consideration.

It was at this point, without discussing it with each other, each determined to apply the law of assumption. It was not until later that each learned what the other had done.

Night after night, they both fell asleep in imagination in the apartment they were considering. The husband, lying with his eyes closed, would imagine that his bedroom windows were overlooking the park. He would imagine going to the window the first thing in the morning and enjoying the view. He felt himself sitting on the terrace overlooking the park, having cocktails with his wife and friends, all thoroughly enjoying it. He filled his mind with actually feeling himself in the penthouse and on the terrace. During all this time, unknown to him, his wife was doing the same thing.

Several weeks went by without any decision on the part of the owners, but they continued to imagine as they fell asleep each night that they were actually sleeping in the penthouse.

One day, to their complete surprise, one of the employees in the apartment building in which they lived told them that the penthouse there was vacant. They were astonished, because theirs was one of the most desirable buildings in the city with a perfect location right on Central Park.

They knew there was a long waiting list of people trying to get an apartment in their building. The fact that a penthouse had unexpectedly become available was kept quiet by the management because they were not in a position to consider any applicants for it.

Upon learning that it was vacant, this couple immediately made a request that it be rented to them, only to be told that this was impossible. The fact was that not only were there several people on a waiting list for a penthouse in the building, but it was actually promised to one family. Despite this, the couple had a series of meetings with the management, at the conclusion of which the apartment was theirs.

The building being subject to rent control, their rental was just about what they had planned to pay when they first started looking for a penthouse.

The location, the apartment itself, and the large terrace surrounding it on the South, West, and North was beyond all their expectations . . and in the living room, on one side, is a giant window 15 feet by 8 feet with a magnificent view of Central Park; one wall is mirrored from floor to ceiling, and there is a wood-burning fireplace.

Neville discusses failure in the attempted use of The Law of Assumption

This book would not be complete without some discussion of failure in the attempted use of The Law of Assumption.

It is entirely possible that you either have had or will have a number of failures in this respect, many of them in really important matters.

If, having read this book, having a thorough knowledge of the application and working of the law of assumption, you faithfully apply it in an effort to attain some intense desire and fail, what is the reason?

If, to the question "Did you persist enough?", you can answer "Yes", and still the attainment of your desire was not realized, what is the reason for failure?

The answer to this, is the most important factor, in the successful use of the law of assumption.

The time it takes your assumption to become fact, your desire to be fulfilled, is directly proportionate to the naturalness of your feeling of already being what you want to be, of already having what you desire.

The fact that it does not feel natural to you, to be what you imagine yourself to be, is the secret of your failure.

Regardless of your desire, regardless of how faithfully and intelligently you follow the law, if you do not feel natural about what you want to be, you will not be it. If it does not feel natural to you to get a better job, you will not get a better job. The whole principle is vividly expressed by the Bible phrase

"you die in your sins"

you do not transcend from your present level
to the state desired.

How can this feeling of naturalness be achieved? The secret lies in one word . . imagination.

For example, this is a very simple illustration:

Assume that you are securely chained to a large heavy iron bench. You could not possibly run, in fact you could not even walk. In these circumstances, it would not be natural for you to run. You could not even feel that it was natural for you to run. But you could easily imagine yourself running.

In that instant, while your consciousness is filled with your imagined running, you have forgotten that you are bound. In imagination, your running was completely natural.

The essential feeling of naturalness can be achieved by persistently filling your consciousness with imagination . . imagining yourself being what you want to be or having what you desire.

Progress can spring only from your imagination, from your desire to transcend your present level. What you truly and literally must feel, is that with your imagination, all things are possible.

You must realize that changes are not caused by caprice, but by a change of consciousness. You may fail to achieve or sustain the particular state of consciousness necessary to produce the effect you desire. But, once you know that consciousness is the only reality and is the sole creator of your particular world and have burnt this truth into your whole being, then you know that success or failure is entirely in your own hands.

Whether or not you are disciplined enough to sustain the required state of consciousness in specific instances has no bearing on the truth of the law itself, that an assumption, if persisted in, will harden into fact.

The certainty of the truth of this law must remain, despite great disappointment and tragedy, even when you

> "see the light of life go out and all the world
> go on as though it were still day".

You must not believe that because your assumption failed to materialize the truth, that assumptions do materialize, is a lie. If your assumptions are not fulfilled, it is because of some error or weakness in your consciousness.

However, these errors and weaknesses can be overcome.

Therefore, press on to the attainment of ever higher levels by feeling that you already are the person you want to be. And remember, that the time it takes your assumption to become reality, is proportionate to the naturalness of being it.

> Man surrounds himself with the true image of himself.
> Every spirit builds itself a house and beyond its
> house a world, and beyond its world a heaven.
> Know then that the world exists for you.
> For you the phenomenon is perfect.
> What we are, that only can we see.

All that Adam had,
all that Caesar could,
you have and can do.
Adam called his house, heaven and earth.
Caesar called his house, Rome;
you perhaps call yours a cobbler's trade;
a hundred acres of land, or a scholar's garret.
Yet line for line and point for point, your dominion is as great
as theirs, though without fine name.
Build therefore your own world.
As fast as you conform your life to the pure idea in your mind,
that will unfold its great proportion.
. . . Emerson

The End

Metaphysical / Law of Attraction Books

David Allen - The Power of I AM (2014), The Power of I AM - Volume 2 (2015), The Power of I AM - Volume 3 (2017)

David Allen - The Creative Power of Thought, Man's Greatest Discovery (2017)

David Allen - The Secrets, Mysteries & Powers of The Subconscious Mind (2017)

David Allen - The Money Bible - The Secrets of Attracting Prosperity (2017)

David Allen - Your Faith Is Your Fortune, Your Unlimited Power

The Neville Goddard Collection (All 10 of his books plus 2 Lecture series) (2016)

Neville Goddard - Assumptions Harden Into Facts: The Book (2016)

Neville Goddard - Imagination: The Redemptive Power in Man (2016)

Neville Goddard - The World is At Your Command - The Very Best of Neville Goddard (2017)

Neville Goddard - Imagining Creates Reality - 365 Mystical Daily Quotes (2017)

Neville Goddard's Interpretation of Scripture (2018)

The Definitive Christian D. Larson Collection (6 Volumes, 30 books) (2014)

SUGGESTED READING

Anthony Norvell - Think Yourself Rich
Charles Fillmore - Prosperity
Charles F. Haanel - The Master Key System
Christian D. Larson, Collection, The Definitive
(6 volume set) (30 Larson books in all)
David Allen - The Power of I AM
David Allen - The Power of I AM - Volume 2
David Allen - The Power of I AM - Volume 3
Ernest Holmes - Creative Mind
Esther Hicks - Abraham - Anything by her
Emmet Fox - The Hidden Power
Florence Scovel Shinn - The Power of the Spoken Word
Florence Scovel Shinn - Your Word is Your Wand
Floyd B. Wilson - Through Silence to Realization
Henry Thomas Hamblin - Dynamic Thought
James Allen - As a Man Thinketh
Joel Goldsmith - Invisible Supply
Joseph Murphy - How To Attract Money
Joseph Murphy - Great Truths That Set Us Free
Joseph Murphy - The Magic of Faith
Joseph Murphy - The Power of Your Subconscious Mind
Joseph Murphy - The Miracles of Your Mind
Joseph Murphy - Within You is the Power
Napoleon Hill - Grow Rich With Peace of Mind
Napoleon Hill - The Master Key to Riches
Napoleon Hill - Think and Grow Rich
Napoleon Hill - You Can Work Your Own Miracles
Neville Goddard - "The Neville Goddard Collection"
(All 10 Books Plus the 1948 Class Lessons and the July 1951 Radio Talks)
Neville Goddard - Your Inner Conversations Are Creating Your World

Neville Goddard's Interpretation of Scripture, Unlocking The Secrets of The Bible
Neville Goddard - Imagination: The Redemptive Power in Man
Neville Goddard - Assumptions Harden Into Facts: The Book
Orison Swett Marden - The Miracle of Right Thought
Prentice Mulford - Thoughts Are Things
Prentice Mulford - Your Forces and How To Use Them
Ralph Waldo Trine - In Tune With The Infinite
Rhonda Byrne - The Secret, The Power, The Magic, The Hero
Robert Collier - Be Rich - The Science Of Getting What You Want
Robert Collier - The Secret of Power
U.S. Andersen - Magic In Your Mind
U.S. Andersen - Three Magic Words
Venice J. Bloodworth - Key To Yourself
Wallace Wattles - The Science of Getting Rich

www.ingramcontent.com/pod-product-compliance
Lightning Source LLC
Chambersburg PA
CBHW021127300426
44113CB00006B/325